August Sarnitz

JOSEF HOFFMANN

1870–1956

In the Realm of Beauty

TASCHEN

HONG KONG KÖLN LONDON LOS ANGELES MADRID PARIS TOKYO

Illustration page 2 ► Josef Hoffmann in Koloman
Moser's studio, approx. 1898
Illustration page 4 ► Design of a wall cabinet,
1899

©2007 TASCHEN GmbH
Hohenzollernring 53, D-50672 Köln
www.taschen.com

Editor ► Peter Gössel, Bremen
Layout ► Gössel und Partner, Bremen
Project management ► Katrin Schumann, Eike
Meyer, Bremen
Text edited by ► Johannes Althoff, Berlin
Translation ► Karl Edward Johnson, Berlin
Editorial coordination ► Johannes Althoff, Berlin

Printed in Germany
ISBN 978-3-8228-5591-1

Contents

6   Introduction

22   Country House for Paul Wittgenstein
24   Vienna Secession VIII Exhibition
26   Double House for Moser and Moll
28   Henneberg Residence
30   Spitzer Residence
32   Vienna Secession XIV Exhibition
34   Wiener Werkstätte
46   Purkersdorf Sanatorium
50   Beer-Hofmann Residence
54   Palais Stoclet
62   Hunting Lodge for Karl Wittgenstein
64   Hochstetter House
66   Kabarett Fledermaus
68   Ast Residence
72   Skywa-Primavesi Residence
76   The Ast Country House
78   Housing Complex Klosehof
82   Sonja Knips Residence
84   Housing Complex Laxenburgerstrasse
86   Row Houses at Werkbund Exhibition
90   Austrian Pavilion at Venice Biennale

92   Life and Work
95   Map
96   Bibliography / Credits / The Author

Introduction

The young Josef Hoffmann

In Vienna no other architect has ever held an artistic and social position comparable to the one held by Josef Hoffmann. He was the celebrated star architect, the embodiment of a new, modern aesthetic, and his list of clients reads like a "Who's Who" of turn-of-the-century Viennese society. His presence was felt in nearly every design-related field—from construction practices to interior design, from exhibition architecture to handcrafted design objects. Among Vienna's intellectual and wealthy upper-class circles, he was regarded as the nearly unchallenged authority whenever aesthetic issues were involved. There is no question that *Kunstwollen*—those creative powers identified by art historian Alois Riegl as the form-giving element of an art period—underwent its personification in Hoffmann.

Josef Hoffmann was deeply convinced of the beneficial powers of beauty. His second wife was a fashion model whose beauty was known all over town. "Beauty," he stressed once, "is the result of centuries of care and ordering ... a part of care is cultivating the inside and outside of a person."

Hoffmann's relationship to beauty harbored traits suggestive of a mania: he found dirt and disorder so distasteful that he had to force himself to study drawings that happened to be spotted. One day an artificial palm tree was placed in the café that he frequented, and when the owner refused to have this affront to the spatial aesthetics removed, Hoffmann immediately sought out a different café. That he especially valued the beauty of hands says a great deal given the fact that he became a pioneer of artistic handicraft: "... men with strenuous professions such as sculptors ... can have hands with a beauty like that of any worker ... For every type of work done with the hands, there must be the right cleansing agent." Hoffmann was equally fussy where touching was involved—a sensitivity with quirk-like characteristics in his case: he had to force himself to shake hands with strangers; he never ate food prepared by people whose hands he found repulsive, and he fled from a room at the sight of fingernails painted red. So, for Hoffmann, what also played a hand in the outcome of any job interview was how the applicant's hands happened to look.

Without much exaggeration, one could hold to the idea that Hoffmann built primarily cultured and up-to-date buildings for up-to-date and cultured people. He was a cultured person himself, a man both up-to-date and modern. His contemporaries were unanimously of the opinion that he personified the "perfect gentleman," "always elegantly dressed, with Homburg and walking stick ..., always surrounded by pretty ladies..." Hoffmann really did seem to attract the ladies. In the classes he taught at the School of Applied Art in Vienna, women were so overproportionately represented—at least for the standards of that time—that his assistant Oswald Haerdtl, who had once reached the end of his tether, complained about "these outrageous chicks making a shambles of the school."

Hoffmann was a reserved and almost shy creature, with a tendency towards mystery-mongering. Simultaneously, his nature revealed a lust for life, kind-heartedness, generosity, and great openness of mind. He was an epicure who sought out the

Left page:
Fruit basket, silver, Wiener Werkstätte, 1904

Design for the interiors published in the magazine *Das Interieur*, 1899

company of others in cafés, bars, and local wine taverns. The rumor circulated throughout Vienna that he invited his employees and friends to Paris on a rollicking excursion and burned up a good deal of the money earned from his principal work, Palais Stoclet.

It remains an undisputed fact that Hoffmann significantly influenced the formation of a modern, aesthetic sensibility and decor, as well as twentieth-century architecture, and did so throughout several phases of their development. Yet, in this very context, he was hardly an intellectual forerunner. He had no taste for theory and flatly refused to explain or analyze his designs. During a radio interview, he said, "There are two types of artists: the ones who develop an idea carefully, sensibly, and systematically, and the ones who just hit on the right idea—I'm more for the ones who hit on things."

If obviously not a man of great words, Hoffmann's visual abilities were brilliant. The people around him were intrigued by his ability to bring to paper an inexhaustible store of forms with the greatest of ease and abandon—even in concert halls. This recalls his remark: "Why should I go to the movies—if I can create something new during the same hour and a half?" What crystallized in Hoffmann's flood of created forms were structures whose recurrence gave them the character of a leitmotif: the isosceles triangle as a tympanum quote, the multiple framing, the vertical fluting for wall surfaces, and others.

Whereas a listing of Hoffmann's complete works is extensive—more than 500 individually cataloged architectural projects and over 1000 design objects—the oeuvre of his writings is easier to order. Hoffmann was a teacher and a good one, but never a so-called art or architecture theorist. Confronted by students asking him what they should do, he advised them in jest: "Go have yourself photographed and duplicated!" Hoffmann's educational maxim was based less on conveying method and more on awakening an artistic personality. In fact, this approach based on solutions arrived at individually also explains why no 'Hoffmann school of thought' could be formed.

Hoffmann categorically rejected intellectual confrontations. Invited one day to give a lecture on art, he refused on the grounds of: "What should you say about art? Make it or leave it alone! There's nothing to talk about, is there?" For Hoffmann, architecture was meant to emerge from an artistic sensibility. "You know, of course, that intelligence and too much knowledge only kill the cultural impulse," Hoffmann wrote to his friend Oskar Kokoschka, adding "...and that only the proper sensibility and the feelings we were born with ever matter."

This artistic sensibility, Hofmann's seismographic sense for locating the height of quality, was used for decades to apprehend aesthetic tendencies and their transformations and rework them, like a catalyst, with an inexhaustible will to design. The poet Richard Beer-Hofmann praised Hoffmann's ability to "remain open to every lively and forward-looking tendency of his day—and simultaneously remain focused on keeping the depths of his soul unspoiled."

In this way, reflected in Hoffmann's lifework are the manifold transformations of the first half of the twentieth century. The designs for his first villas exist under the spell of the Scottish Arts and Crafts movement. Mackintosh's influence led to his using a strict, geometric, and almost abstract formal language, during the course of which he arrived at the recurring cubical forms and patterns later to function like leitmotifs in his creative output. As early as 1902, his formalism led to his first abstract project: two overdoor reliefs made of carved mortar, completed for the Secession XIV exhibition in Vienna, an

artistic step without consequences. The same could be said about his Palais Stoclet in Brussels, nevertheless Hoffmann's principal work, becoming an Art Nouveau icon. In the years preceding World War I, he completed buildings such as Skywa-Primavesi Residence and the Austrian House for the German Werkbund Exhibition in Cologne (1914), both clearly under the sign of neoclassicism. Yet a decade later, he completed designs in French Art Deco style. Throughout all the different periods and transformations, however, Hoffmann realized houses—mostly in rural settings—which, like Villa Böhler in Karpfenberg, in the Styria region, were so well-adapted to the respective local traditions that they hardly differed from their surroundings. Most significantly, Hoffmann was the ideal architect for finishing work and rebuilding, especially for projects involving discreet additions to existing historical structures. In such instances, as in the case of Böhler's country house in Baden near Vienna, Hoffmann created astounding, formal approximations that should never be mistaken for imitations.

This chameleonic characteristic led to Hoffmann remaining an important representative of Austrian architecture long after the break from 1918 onward and the radical social changes connected with it. Eventually, following World War II, and due largely to the increasing popularity of 'rationalism', his total work of art approach, his preference for handwork and ornamentation was frowned upon. Hoffmann, who had set the pace until then, suddenly found himself overshadowed by new developments and dropped out of sight. It was only in the 1970s—through a turning away from functionalism and the embracing of postmodernism—that Hoffmann was rediscovered and since then considered one of the most important idea and impetus-giving sources in the world of modern design.

This rediscovery is not least of all due to the fact that Josef Hoffmann had an antidogmatic nature and led people, as it were, towards their own individual freedom.

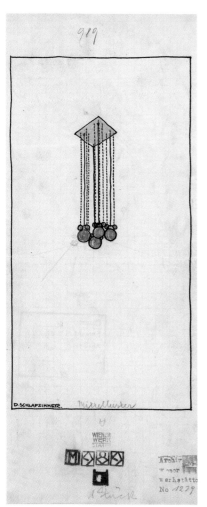

Chandelier design for a woman's bedroom, 1908

Also, Hoffmann's status is unique among twentieth-century architects: viewed from the standpoint of his turning away from historicism, he was among the forerunners of the Modern on the one hand, and simultaneously among the forerunners of those who overcame the Modern on the other—which he accomplished by rejecting functionalism, the *Nutzstil*, his teacher Otto Wagner represented. Indeed, Hoffmann did take on Wagner's respect for materials and currentness, architecture and design, however, were altogether good and properly freed of their function, which he replaced with artistic intention. In this way, as an artist, Hoffmann assumed the role of mediator for a territory that was absolutely staged and founded on ideas.

With the artist-architect as mediator of beauty, the renewal of architecture and art understood in this light occurred, so to speak, "from top to bottom" and was not only meant to penetrate and ennoble all areas of life—including those areas related to daily activities—but also to grant life a greater glory in the process. For this reason Hoffmann never made a distinction between an artwork and an object for everyday use, and this soon opened up the rift between himself and Adolf Loos, who later became his opponent. For the author of the essay *Ornament and Crime*, the elevating of objects for everyday use to 'ennobled' artworks—meaning here objects produced using handwork or antiquated production methods—was no less superfluous than applying an ornament. The conflict here was of a fundamental nature: while Loos advocated the position of a fundamental renewal in the sense of an ethical strategy, in the case of Hoffmann it was necessary to speak of an aesthetic attitude. Hoffmann was after all 'medium' for contacting the *Kunstwollen* or art-desiring impulse of his time—an impulse that had meanwhile entered into a dialogue with the "wish for art" as expressed by Vienna's self-confident bourgeoisie, a class forever striving to give adequate expression to its elevated social and political standing. For the members of this privileged class, ornamentation was perfectly legitimate as long as it was new. At the close of the Danube monarchy, as this class lost its political and social importance to an increasing degree, it also happened that Hoffmann's star began to gradually wane.

Josef Hoffmann was born on December 15, 1870, in Pirnitz (Brtnice) near Iglau, in the region of Moravia—only five days after his opponent-to-be, Adolf Loos, first saw the

Otto Wagner (left), Josef Hoffmann, Otto Prutscher, and Koloman Moser in front of a café in Vienna, approx. 1903

light of day some fifty miles away in the town of Brünn. Hoffmann came from a well-situated, thoroughly middle-class family. His father was co-owner of a local cotton manufacturer as well as mayor of his small town. For his pre-college training, the young Hoffmann attended the same school in Iglau that Adolf Loos attended. Hoffmann's parents expected their son to study law and later pursue a civil service career. To their dismay, however, his grades were below average, and with every repetition of the fifth year of grammar school things went worse for Hoffmann: "It was an agonizing disgrace," he would say later. "It left me embittered all throughout my youth. Even today it gives me a certain minority complex [sic]." It was only after discovering his interest in architecture that Hoffmann made good, beginning his studies in the construction department of the state school of applied arts in 1887 and obtaining his college entrance qualification in 1891.

In 1892, when Josef Hoffmann began his architecture studies at the Academy of Fine Arts in Vienna, he first studied under Carl Freiherr von Hasenauer, at the peak of his career then as one of the 'Ringstrasse' architects, and afterwards under Otto Wagner, the forerunner of 'modern architecture,' who later wrote a treatise of the same

Garden façade of Charles R. Mackintosh's Hill House in Helensburgh, 1902–1903

name. In 1894, in the first speech delivered by Wagner after assuming his post, he proclaimed his turning away from the prevailing historicism: "Art and artists should and must represent their own day and age. Our future salvation cannot consist of merely mimicking all the stylistic tendencies that flourished over the last decades ... Art, in its nascence, must be imbued with the realism of our present time."

Soon Hoffmann belonged to the inner circle of Wagner students and work colleagues who played a major role in the emergence of Viennese modernism. Also around this time, Hoffmann's friendship with Joseph Maria Olbrich developed. In 1895 Hoffmann and others with similar interests, among them Olbrich, Koloman Moser, and Carl Otto Czeschka, founded the elitist "Sevener's Club," a forerunner of Vienna Secession. This was the forum for the avant-garde, this was the place to be for discussing new tendencies in art. Presumably here too is where Hoffmann first heard of William Morris and the Arts and Crafts movement that Morris founded in early nineteenth-century Great Britain as both a counter movement to conventional mass-production methods born of the industrial age and a way to revive the handwork-related crafts trade.

However, during this period it was not possible for Hoffmann to keep historicism entirely bound up. The independently developed design submitted as his final project during his last year of study under Otto Wagner, for which he chose as its motto *Forum orbis, insula pacis* (Forum of the World, Island of Peace), was an ambitious work at the same time formally linked to Renaissance style. Praised by Wagner as a masterpiece, this design earned Hoffmann the prestigious "Rome Prize," which financed a period of study in Italy.

Josef Hoffmann and Fritz Wärndorfer with the first silver article produced by Wiener Werkstätte, 1903

After returning from Italy, Hoffmann set off to work in Otto Wagner's architecture office. In the same year he became one of the founding members of the *Vereinigung bildender Künstler Österreichs* named the "Secession," enabling him greater contact with artistic circles and, most of all, with wealthy members of Vienna's high society interested in culture. Among other projects, he completed the installation designs for the first 'Secession' exhibitions and designed the anteroom and secretary's office of the Secession Building—all highly significant tasks for Vienna's Avant-garde art market.

Also in 1897, an essay by Hoffmann entitled "The Architecture of the Island of Capri" appeared in the magazine *Der Architekt*, which turned out to be a programmatic manifesto: "What works perfectly here [on Capri] is the flat simplicity of what appear to be painting-inspired construction ideas—none of them artistically weighed down by bad decorations ... The folk art, which truly flourishes in these simple country houses, has a tremendous effect on any unbiased nature, and it repeatedly reminds us of what we lack at home ... Consider the example set by Capri ... not to emulate this other construction method but rather to awaken in ourselves a warm and homey lifestyle concept, not geared to de-decoration practices based on poorly-conceived frameworks with laughable, factory made and cast-cement ornaments, or an imposed Swiss gable-fronted house architecture ... instead, to awaken a lifestyle concept geared to creating simple, sympathetic, atmospheric, and uniformed groupings endowed with natural colors. Here too, while the wealth of details would preferably be kept to a minimum, they would also be the likes of sculptures and custom-made by real artists ... In this

Josef Hoffmann at a building site, 1903

Above:
Street façade of the Palais Stoclet, Brussels
1905–1911

Entrance of the Wiener Werkstätte sales
outlet, Am Graben, Vienna 1907

area, England has made greater advancements than we have. Should England's for the
most part Middle-Ages-derived forms prove unsubstantial for our needs, we should
nevertheless remain aware of England's interest in the Arts and Crafts and in art in
general, and evoke that spirit here at home—by repeatedly searching our souls for our
own forms, and finally by pushing away from ourselves with force the last strains of an
obsolete, inebriated mix-up of styles."

These sentences are proof of Hoffmann's spiritual independence: the turning away
from a historicism emptied of meaning was not to import new models as replace-
ments for those just rejected; instead, the main concern here was to establish contact
with a lively, local tradition. In this sense, the Tudor style upheld by the Arts and Crafts
movement could hardly serve as a source of inspiration now, whereas the search for
one's own roots and striving to ennoble daily existence with art really could inspire—
for which the reorganization of the artistic handicrafts was paramount. The essential

element of Josef Hoffmann's modernism was based on the founding of a new identity, which took into account the given technical options. The greatest goal of all was to conceive of a new harmony which would essentially manifest itself in the sense of a total work of art. The materials' authenticity, a consistently conceived decor, and a construction style well-adapted to the site would all play an exceptional role—in serving an up-to-date and lifestyle-oriented culture for whose realization Hoffmann therefore recommended an art-loving, modern, and wealthy upper-class public.

In 1899, only four years after completing his studies and now twenty-nine years old, Hoffmann was awarded a professorship at the School of Applied Arts in Vienna. In 1900 he was chosen to create the installation design for the school's exhibition spaces at the Paris World's Fair which could be regarded as a national and international acknowledgement.

That same year, Hoffmann completed the installation design for the exhibition spaces of Vienna Secession VIII, one of the most important shows ever dedicated to the

Small basket for confectionery, approx. 1905

Berlin branch of the Wiener Werkstätte, 1929

theme of Arts and Crafts. From Paris came "Maison Moderne," founded by Julius Meier-Graefe; from Belgium Henry van de Velde; from London, with his 'Guild of Handicraft,' Charles R. Ashbee, and from Glasgow the husband-and-wife artists couples Mackintosh and McNair. This show would immediately affect Hoffmann's work. The villas that he completed in Vienna on 'Hohe Warte'—a picturesque residential area located on a crest and overlooking wine vineyards and the famous Vienna Woods—were visibly influenced by the Arts and Crafts movement. This was evident in their structural frameworks, windows divided into square units, high-pitched roofs, and well-ordered garden designs, as well as their entranceway areas built in the tradition of English "halls".

Over the following years, Hoffman's designs attained a greater simplicity and stringency. His motifs became dominated by geometric forms. It was around this time too, that he developed his preference for using the square in his work, and earned the nickname "Hoffmann Squared". Looking back on that particular period of his develop-

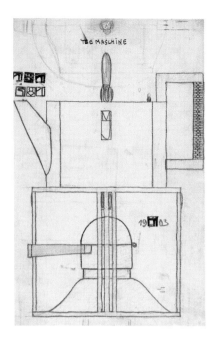

Design for a samovar

ment, he explained that he was "so interested in the square and black-and-white tones because these clear elements never appeared in earlier styles ..."

The sopraporta reliefs Hoffmann created in 1902 for the Secession XIV exhibition mark the height of this puritanical phase. This exhibition served to present the Beethoven statue by the Leipzig sculptor Max Klinger. Around this artwork, Vienna's Secessionist artists created unified artistic surroundings with the intention of realizing here their ideal of a *Gesamtkunstwerk*, or *total work of art*. The term *Gesamtkunstwerk* dates back to Richard Wagner, whose text *Das Kunstwerk der Zukunft* (The Artwork of the Future), published in 1850, extols the notion of reuniting what was originally a single art but now divided into different artistic genres. "This great, universal work of art" synthesizes all the art genres, and its goal is to represent human nature in its entirety—moreover, "this great, universal work of art cannot be recognized [by the artist] as being the arbitrary act of a single individual but rather as a necessary, conceivable and mutual work of a future mankind."

Intrinsically linked to this ideal was the enterprise that Hoffmann and his two friends, the painter Kolo Moser and the industrialist Fritz Wärndorfer, launched almost a year after Secession XIV: the "Wiener Werkstätte Produktivgenossenschaft von Kunsthandwerkern in Wien" (Vienna Workshops). During the approximately thirty years of the workshops' existence, they doubled as the "interior decorating company"

Samovar with stand and burner, 1903

Austrian Pavilion, Rome 1910–1911

for Hoffmann's projects, allowing him to furnish entire apartments and houses independent of outside firms. The inspirational models for this enterprise were naturally the Arts and Crafts movement and the Guild of Handicraft. In 1924, in an essay printed in *Kunstblatt*, entitled *Die Schule des Architekten* ("The Architect's School"), Hoffmann divulged the ideal he had in mind during the founding of the Wiener Werkstätte: "In the Middle Ages there was a stonemason's lodge, certainly the most ideal type of building school ... here you found all the artists and handwork specialists needed to construct a building. What this union ensured for all involved was an artistic sensibility of the same kind; in fact, it ensured a style ... The fact that everyone involved knew each other through and through guaranteed the style's proper application, and the mutual appreciation of all the rendered services, in all the respective fields, led to the enthusiastic commitment on the part of each individual for the good of the common cause. An artisan locksmith was valued as highly as a painter or a sculptor; a stonemason as highly as a carpenter; the goldsmith as respected as the creator of ornaments, and the weaver of tapestries was as respected as the painter of miniatures ... Only quality mattered—not a biased ordering of rank."

The first years of collaboration with the Wiener Werkstätte mark the peak of Hoffmann's creative output: the 34-year-old architect and designer completes the Purkersdorf Sanatorium (1904–1905), already considered a mature work, and produces all the sanatorium's furnishings together with the Wiener Werkstätte. Hoffmann's principal work, however, is unambiguously the magnificent Palais Stoclet in Brussels, which he begins working on a year later. With an almost unlimited amount of money at his disposal, what could be erected in Brussels was an exceptional *Gesamtkunstwerk*—a 'total work of art' in which the structure's opulence and wealth of artistry unfold on an almost Baroque scale in order to create an atmospheric spatial symphony with a staggering array of colors and materials. For the rest of his life Hoffmann would be measured against this architectural feat completed in 1911. Palais

Below:
Goblet with curlicue handles, brass, approx. 1925

Stoclet represents the height of cultural refinement as it existed in Europe before World War I. Ranked among the greatest architectural designs of the twentieth century, Palais Stoclet is on a par with the Villa Savoye by Le Corbusier, the Barcelona Pavilion by Mies van der Rohe, and the Fallingwater House by Frank Lloyd Wright.

Josef Hoffmann belongs to a generation of architects for whom the embracing of the Arts and Crafts movement was linked with artistic liberation. The connecting of interior architecture design with the overall construction altered the standard and the period reference: experimentation, diversity of form, and momentum shifted more into the area of design—while the actual architecture forfeits a portion of its dynamic and becomes a space for housing handcrafted products.

The transition to neoclassicism is already apparent in the Austrian Pavilion for Rome (1910–1911), visible through the symmetrical ordering of the exhibition area

Large exhibition hall of the Austrian Pavilion
at the International Arts and Crafts Exhibition,
Paris 1925

around an almost quadratic forecourt. At the court-bearing side of the structure, both side wings are headed by pillared porticos whose fluted pillars have neither foundation nor capital. Created two years later was the neo-Palladian country house for Otto Primavesi (1913–1914), executed as a wood-brick building, with a two-story portico. In this structure, the formal folkloric elements are poetically combined within a strict architectural arrangement. Here the innovative aspect is unifying two seemingly incompatible design attitudes. Also notable here—typical of Hoffmann—is having the design create the period reference and guarantee the artistic intention's relevance, while the architecture addresses the historical permanence of the country house.

This fundamental embracing of neoclassicism manifested itself in creations which secured Hoffmann's reputation as an advertising vehicle for modern Austria: the Austrian House at the German Werkbund Exhibition in Cologne (1914) qualifies as an

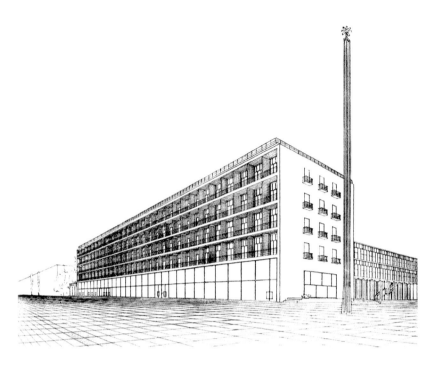

Mocha pot and milk dispenser, approx. 1933
Executed by J. C. Klinkosch

impressive example of monumental, pillared architecture utilizing a centralized inner courtyard. The same applies to the residence for Josefine Skywa and Robert Primavesi, completed around the same time in Vienna (1913–1915), a building whose façade facing the street conveys an accentuated classicist expression through two lateral, gabled areas, between which stand four pillared columns. Here too, one experiences 'modernism' in the details of the interior architecture—in the salon's interior space, and the auxiliary building forming the small teahouse. Two more examples of this would be the city villa for Sonja Knips (1924–1925) and the Austrian Pavilion featured at the Art and Crafts Exhibition in Paris (1925).

Hoffmann had no way of avoiding the new debates on architecture which developed during the 1920s, especially those in connection with publications such as *Der moderne Zweckbau* (The Modern Functional Building) by Adolf Behne and *International Architecture* by Walter Gropius. As early as 1907, he had already met Le Corbusier in Vienna and, at the latest, knew his work from the Arts and Crafts Exhibition in Paris (1925), where Le Corbusier presented his "L'Esprit nouveau" pavilion. In 1927 Hoffmann visited the Werkbund exhibition in Stuttgart. Among other projects, he viewed Le Corbusier's double house in the Weissenhof housing settlement, and his "Citrohan" house. Yet in Hoffmann's own works a corresponding reception of "international architecture" was slow to take hold. The draft he submitted in conjunction with a competition focused on building a hotel in Vienna (1927) reveals a radical design based on a skeletal construction. While the walls on the ground floor are completely glazed, the upper story is given a combination balcony and gallery. But Hoffmann never again reached this project's level of modernism in his later constructions.

Following the housing complex on Laxenburgerstrasse (1928–1932) and his contribution to the housing colony developed by the Viennese Werkbund (1930–1932), it was clear by now that Hoffmann had outlived his day. As it was, the Viennese Werkbund's exhibition had already documented Austria's becoming unhitched from current developments in the area of modern architecture, made obvious by the fact that the show first opened on June 4, 1932, literally months after the epoch-making exhibition "The International Style" was shown at the Museum of Modern in New York—a 'delay' that could be seen as symptomatic of Austrian modernism, and conducted without an institutionalized discourse.

In all his life, Hoffmann lived and worked in territories that existed in a world parallel to reality—socially, artistically, economically, and politically speaking. His access to this parallel world was made possible through sophisticated upper-class patrons who represented a new social class. These people wanted to see themselves as proudly representing a class to itself and moreover, they wanted to see their ideal of a paradise on earth become a reality. These were the people who enabled a departure towards new artistic dimensions through the construction of buildings such as Purkersdorf Sanatorium and Palais Stoclet—and the same people who supported new social and economic approaches of the type pursued by Wiener Werkstätte. Yet Hoffmann's obliging nature towards his clients went hand in hand with a noncommittal attitude towards his own design creations. By never resolving the pressing issues which arose in this respect, he eventually lost himself in the realm of things beautiful. In the 1930s, however, the moment of truth finally arrived: the workshops of the Wiener Werkstätte were liquidated in 1932, and later, in 1936, when Hoffmann reached retirement age, passionate teacher that he was he could only accept with bitterness being told by the administrators of the School of Applied Arts that they saw no reason to keep him on the payroll.

Over the next years, particularly after World War II, Hoffmann completed only a few projects. Viewed from their core, his late works function like commentaries on the respective tendencies of their time. A characteristic example of this would be his almost rococo-like interpretation of the late modern age as expressed in a design for the "d'une grand vedette" boudoir at the 1937 Paris World's Fair. Set on a floor covered with mirrored plates, one sees a white angora carpet and seating with floral-patterned upholstery and silver-coated wooden feet. That sections of the walls are mirrored as well causes a dematerializing effect in the space. What also shines through here is the well-known, individual design attitude which brings Hoffmann's ideas closer to those for a Hollywood film set.

Hoffmann's importance lies in his impetus-giving function for a design not determined by functional necessity—a design as the articulation of cultural and social issues—and the reverse: a design as the visualization of unconscious issues. In this respect, Hoffmann is the most 'Viennese' of the modern architects: he gave form to the soul's desires.

"Boudoir d'une grande vedette" exhibition room at the Paris World's Fair, 1937

1899·Country House for Paul Wittgenstein
Bergerhöhe near Hohenberg, Lower Austria

"I hope that for us too, the day will come when wall paper, painted ornaments for ceilings, as well as furniture and objects for everyday use can all be ordered through an artist instead of a dealer." Only two years would pass before this hope, expressed by Josef Hoffmann in 1897, was finally realized. In 1899 he was commissioned by the industrialist Paul Wittgenstein to rebuild his country house 'Bergerhöhe' nearby Hohenberg in Lower Austria. A family of Jewish descent converted to Protestant faith, the Wittgensteins were Austria's leading producers of steel and often called the Austrian Krupps. Not only financially did they belong to the country's elite; the same applied on a intellectual level. Paul Wittgenstein, uncle of philosopher Ludwig Wittgenstein and director of the St. Aegyd Ironworks, had a strong interest in literature and the arts. He came to meet Hoffmann through his close ties with members of the Vienna Secession.

In July 1899 permission was granted to begin rebuilding the country house, with the work most likely completed that same year. Although this involved a relatively simple task, Hoffmann was nevertheless free to handle the design as he wished and enjoyed his client's complete trust.

"Das Haus des Friedes in Stille" (House of Peace in Tranquility)—this quote by Luther, adorning the entranceway, epitomized the architecture. Externally, the house scarcely stands out in the immediate surroundings. However, its interior spaces combine a rural tastefulness, not to be mistaken for a common rural aesthetic, with an avant-garde and international modernism. The living room and bedroom, with bordering bathroom, convey the kind of aesthetic liveliness produced by swung shapes which Art Nouveau style became known for. All the furniture was designed by Hoffmann, with the extended arch between the two rooms masterfully accentuated by the built-in furniture. As an Art Nouveau ornament, painted shapes are stenciled on the walls; these appear throughout all the rooms and form a color-coordinated unity with the reddish-orange curtains. The overall color scheme of the furnishings expresses here a cultivated modesty.

Paul Wittgenstein would feel obliged to Hoffmann for the rest of his life. Later, Wittgenstein not only commissioned him to build a Protestant village church in St. Aegyd am Neuwald, but also to handle the interior of his city apartment in Vienna.

1900 ▸ Vienna Secession VIII Exhibition
Friedrichstrasse 12, Vienna I

**Cover of the Secession VIII
exhibition catalog**

In 1897 Hoffmann was a founding member of the "Vereinigung bildender Künstler Österreichs," an organization of Austrian artists named the "Secession". Both in part and in full, he designed many of the Secession's exhibition spaces, and Secession VIII exhibition—designed by Josef Hoffmann, Koloman Moser, and Leopold Bauer—plays a major role in the development of modernism in Vienna. It focuses on the presentation of the Arts and Crafts movement with special attention given to works by artists and architects from England and Scotland. On this occasion, Hoffmann displayed a large number of his own creations—handcrafted design objects and furniture—whose simple and strict designs divulge the influence of British models.

In the catalog's introductory text, the curators stressed that the "Arts and Crafts movement purses the same goal in all the nations of the world: *to give moderne sensibility the corresponding form*. In the process, what typifies a nationality is brought to light. Works from abroad are not meant to act as models which our creations at home try to copy but rather as measuring instruments for our own abilities." While major developments in Great Britain's Arts and Crafts movement were made known on the European continent through the magazine *The Studio*, simultaneously the revival of the Arts and Crafts movement in Austria, and founding of the Austrian Museum of Art and Industry, were directly inspired by English models such as the Victoria & Albert Museum in London.

This explains the enormous interest shown for the objects and furniture designs exhibited by Charles Robert Ashbee and the artist couple Mackintosh and Herbert McNair. Charles Rennie Mackintosh (1868–1928) was only two years older than Josef Hoffmann and, at the age of twenty-nine, won the competition to design the building for the Glasgow School of Art, erected from 1898 to 1909. Mackintosh became famous for his uniquely designed tearoom interiors in Glasgow, for stringent forms based on the square, and for lines extended vertically into the heights, everything developed above and beyond a real function. For the Secession VIII exhibition, Mackintosh and his wife Margaret created a sensational tearoom. On this occasion, both husband and wife traveled to Vienna, where they were enthusiastically received. What their visit also confirmed was that Vienna Secession could now be understood as an international address for art discourse.

Hoffmann was so impressed with Mackintosh's work that, during his stay in London in 1902, he arranged for a detour to Glasgow in order to visit him. In Vienna, the opportunity often arose in which he 'combined' his own furniture designs with those by Mackintosh. Not much later, though, works such as the high-backed side chairs for the Flöge Fashion Salon in Wien-Mariahilf (1904) nevertheless show that Hoffmann quickly developed his own designs independent of the British models. While exhibitions on the scale of Secession VIII were obviously inspirational for artists, the idea of them causing an immediate dependency was out of the question.

Left page:
Middle hall of the Secession VIII Exhibition

1900–1901▸Double House for Moser and Moll

Steinfeldgasse 6–8, Vienna XIX

Garden façade of double house for Kolo Moser (left) and Carl Moll (right)

The double house Hoffmann created for his friends Koloman Moser and Carl Moll marked the beginning of what would become the "Hohe Warte Artists' Colony" in the Wien-Döbling area. The project's initiator, Carl Moll, entrusted Hoffmann with work already started by Joseph Olbrich but never completed because of Olbrich's move to Darmstadt. Hoffmann's clients were both painters and, like himself, founding members of Vienna Secession. Kolo Moser (1868–1918) was married to Ditha Mautner von Markhof, the daughter of an industrialist; he founded the Wiener Werkstätte (Vienna Workshops) together with Josef Hoffmann in 1903. Carl Moll (1861–1945) organized the first Wiener Werkstätte exhibition in the gallery he directed, Galerie Miethke; his stepdaughter, Alma Schindler, who lived in the house for a brief period, later became famous through her marriages to different well-known artists: Alma Mahler-Werfel.

That Hoffmann drew his inspiration for the double house from the Arts and Crafts movement is made apparent in the pointed gables and the upper story's latticework. Although the part of the house for Moser is smaller than the one for Moll, their ground

26

plans share a similar matrix: in both halves of the house, kitchen, servants' quarters and other side rooms are located in the basement. Due to the slope of the property, this basement nearly functions like a full story where it faces the street. In turn, the side of the second story facing the street functions more like a first story, and like a ground-floor level where it faces the garden. Both halves of the house are provided with their own spacious hall, living room, dining room, bedroom, and an attic, meant for use as a studio. The larger part of the Moll House has additional bedrooms.

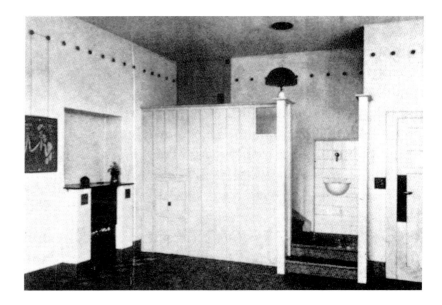

Right:
Living hall of Moser's house
View toward staircase

Street façade of Moser's house with bay window

In both halves of the house, the architectural staging of the living hall with the flight of stairs plays a major role. In the houses for Henneberg and Spitzer, this arrangement is further developed to a two-story living hall. Originally, the houses were characterized by strong textures and contrasts resulting from the interplay of their rough plaster, sheet metal, painted wooden surfaces, and tall brick-colored roofs. All the windows and doors are divided into square modules—a motif, which, in Hoffmann's later constructions, altogether displaces the façade design based on English models.

The fact that the building's aesthetic-ethical dimensions strive to achieve here a "moral" and "sincere" architecture, the founding spirit of the Wiener Werkstätte, which unites both the clients and architect, is given a voice of its own in the double house—a spirit not least of all reflected in the maxim which praises the unifying of a house and its furnishings in the sense of creating a total work of art, "...a house," says Hoffmann, "whose exterior is obliged to divulge its interior."

1900–1901 ▸ Henneberg Residence
Wollergasse 8, Vienna XIX

Street view, approx. 1901

Ground plan of first floor (parterre)

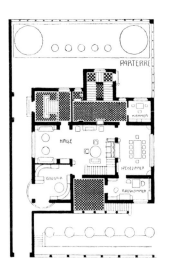

Following the Moser-Moll double house, Henneberg's residence was the second building added to "Hohe Warte Artists' Colony". Here too, the influence of the Arts and Crafts movement is detectable in Hoffmann's work. The façades' upper story displays a combination of plastered masonry and timber framework leading directly into the roof construction. The combining of pointed roof forms with flat roofs and terraces of a Mediterranean stamp connects the medieval elements to those of the classical period. This already announces a turning away from the English models and from swung forms in favor of the cubical design soon to be fully exploited by Hoffmann.

This development is particularly evident in the living hall with which Hoffmann realized for the first time the innovative spatial configuration that his larger residential buildings would be known for. Here spatial volume, spatial height, movement, staircase situation, lighting, building materials, furniture, coloring, and artworks are combined to form a unified spatial choreography, celebrated enthusiastically by the critics as flowing motion and continuity of sequence of spaces. The two-story living hall is a multifunctional space, a stage on which living is performed, as well as a pivotal area from which the entire house connects to a dining room, boudoir, and terrace. This made the house the ideal backdrop for representing an art-loving, Viennese upper-class boldly striving to distinguish itself from the traditional nobility.

Large two-floor living hall with fireplace and Gustav Klimt's portrait of Marie Henneberg

Garden view with pergola

Hugo Henneberg was a wealthy art lover and art photographer. He felt drawn to Secession-related thought and organized exhibitions of his own works in both the Secession's exhibition spaces and in the Hagenbund. In 1888 he embarked on a study trip throughout the United States; he collected Japanese woodcuts and enthusiastically followed international developments in the art world. The portrait that Gustav Klimt painted of Henneberg's wife was hung in the living hall of the new house axially facing the entrance, so that, upon entering the house, every visitor felt received by Marie Henneberg herself.

In the smoking room, Hennenberg's worldly taste in art was emphasized by the presence of an exquisite closet designed by Charles Mackintosh from Glasgow. The photography studio with darkroom was located in the attic, and a protruding terrace offered a breathtaking view of the Vienna Woods.

Severly damaged during World War II, the house was later rebuilt as an apartment building. Today practically nothing remains of Hoffmann's original design.

1901–1902 ▸ Spitzer Residence
Steinfeldgasse 4, Vienna XIX

Together with the Moser-Moll double house and Henneberg's residence in the immediate vicinity, the villa for Friedrich Victor Spitzer, also built in the prestigious Hohe Warte area, belongs just as much to the first group of architectural works created by Hoffmann.

Elements of the Arts and Crafts movement characterize the considerably subdivided structure. The façade facing the street shows a magnificent house with an entrance enhanced by a projecting porch-like structure, while a spacious terrace on the second story divides the body of the house centrically. By comparison, the façade facing the garden remains virtually windowless, which further emphasizes the structural division of the house. Here it is visible that the architect changed his direction towards a more cubical design, towards a greater simplicity and stringency.

The house owner's photography studio was placed behind an oversized bay window. Spitzer was an enthusiastic photographer and a member of the famous "Camera

Street view, approx. 1902

Spacious two-floor living hall, with open fireplace made of lead and copper, and a large ceiling light made of metal and glass
The walls are fitted with black-stained wooden paneling, above which is grainy white plaster.

Ground plan of first floor (parterre)

Club," as his two neighbors Hugo Henneberg and Baron Nathaniel Rothschild were. Also like Henneberg, Spitzer too, was drawn to Secession-related thought and exhibited his photographic works in the Secession's exhibition spaces as well as in the Hagenbund.

The 16.40-foot-high ceiling and 645.8 square feet of floor area of the living hall in Spitzer's house is as famous as the one in Henneberg's residence. In effect, what is developed here is the notion of a Viennese interpretation of the English living hall, with an fireplace and connecting staircase. This multifunctional space was used as a fireplace room, library, and music room, and it featured a platform that served as a concert podium.

An interesting feature of the interior decoration of the house is the juxtapositioning of the furniture designed by Hoffmann and the previously commissioned furniture designed by Joseph Olbrich, both for Spitzer. With regard to their cubical forms, perfectly coordinated with the geometric ornaments that appear in the upholstery and carpets, the designs in Spitzer's residence have a special artistic value. Compared with earlier designs a conscious reduction to the square as a basic form becomes visible. "For Viennese standards this creates an interesting art history contrast," notes critic Ludwig Hevesi, judging the space and its furnishings in his book *Altkunst—Neukunst* (Old Art—New Art). "A connoisseur's space in the forms and colors emerging from Olbrich's fantasy on the one hand, and the space of a strict, logic-ridden lover of good taste on the other—Hoffmann, with his own unique way of using so little to create so much."

Spitzer remained owner of the house until 1919, after which time the house continually changed owners, so that now the original division of the interior spaces is gone. Today the villa nevertheless exists in a well-preserved state; its modifications have been in part reversed with the original structure restored, and the building is now classified as a historical monument.

1902 ▸ Vienna Secession XIV Exhibition
Friedrichstrasse 12, Vienna I

Beethoven frieze by Gustav Klimt (detail)

In the area of exhibition development, Hoffmann's perhaps greatest achievement was his installation design and overall artistic direction for Secession XIV—an exhibition held in 1902 and dedicated to the presentation of a Beethoven statue created by Leipzig artist Max Klinger. Within the German-language cultural realm, this represented an epoch-making, turn-of-the-century event: for nearly two and a half months, from April 15 to June 27, the Secession Building created by Joseph Maria Olbrich and located on Wienzeile became a center of cult worship for the composer Ludwig van Beethoven.

During the preparations for the exhibition the design approach was reversed: "First create a uniform space, then enhance it with paintings and sculptures that effectively serve the spatial concept." Hoffmann's main concern was to give the exhibition spaces "the character of monumentality." Consequently, he chose to "hold firmly to a great simplicity in the materials used and formal language." What he created was a three-aisled spatial ordering. In the center of the main hall with its firmament-like barrel vault stood the polychrome statue of Beethoven made of marble and bronze, depicting the composer as an Olympian god, his posture strained, the expression on his face concentrated yet energetic, and his fists clenched. Behind the figure, displayed on the back wall, was Alfred Roller's mural *Die sinkende Nacht* (Sinking Night), symbolizing the decline of the past. The figure's gaze was directed towards the front of the space, where Adolf Böhm's mural *Der werdende Tag* (The Approaching Day) symbolized the departure into a new future.

**Max Klinger's Beethoven sculpture in the
main hall of the Secession Exhibition**
For this exhibition, Hoffmann specially installed a
firmament-like barrel vault under the glass ceiling.

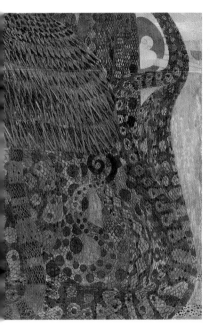

The central room was flanked by two aisles given flat ceilings and lit with skylights. These were the spaces decorated with murals thematically related to Beethoven's Ninth Symphony: in the aisle on the left, to which the visitor was firstly directed in preparation for the actual event, was the *Beethoven Frieze* by Gustav Klimt; in the aisle on the right, forming the visual conclusion, the wall surfaces were designed by a variety of artists. Openings in the walls of both aisles allowed the Beethoven statue to be gazed at. Hoffmann installed his own work above both doorways leading from the aisles into the central room: sopraporta reliefs composed of abstract, rectangular elements made of carved mortar. The ideal of the total work of art was fully attained when Gustav Mahler performed in these spaces his arrangement for wind instruments with motifs from the closing chorus of the Ninth Symphony.

Reflected in this staging was the conception of the Secessionists: Beethoven, the epitome of the artist, was celebrated as the embodiment of mankind's genius, which, by overcoming its fate, allows mankind's creative spirit to throw off its shackles and, in doing so, rescues mankind—with the Ninth Symphony, regarded as the manifestation of this heroic act, as the highest revelation in art.

**Side-hall exit with Josef Hoffmann's "abstract"
sopraporta reliefs**

In point of fact, the Wiener Werkstätte (Vienna Workshops) should be counted among Josef Hoffmann's 'major works'. Although the copyrights of its diverse products were owned by different artists, Hoffmann was after all the dominating personality, guiding spirit, and soul of this undertaking. Among others the British Arts and Crafts Movement served as a model for the Wiener Werkstätte. Hoffmann remembered the founding of the Wiener Werkstätte as follows: „One afternoon at lunchtime we all sat in the Heinrichshof Café, Otto Wagner, Kolo Moser, some friends, and, more importantly, Fritz Wärndorfer. ... Moser and I were busy cursing the state of the arts scene in Vienna. To us, Vienna appeared to be in a state of dilapidation and rotten, whereas everywhere else in Europe consciousness arose. ... Everywhere but in Vienna workshops were founded with the aim to put an end to the perennial imitation of styles long passed, trying to find new shapes, appropriate for our modern times. Profoundly accusing this dull era with all its impossibilities, one of the gentlemen, who had just returned to Vienna after his sojourn in London and whom we only knew slightly, mentioned that it wouldn't even cost the price of a house trying something similar in Vienna." In May 1903, the enterprise was entered in Vienna's commercial trade register

Reception area and showroom of the Wiener Werkstätte, Neustiftgasse, Vienna, approx. 1903

Right:
Stationery set, approx. 1910
Ebony with mother-of-pearl veneer

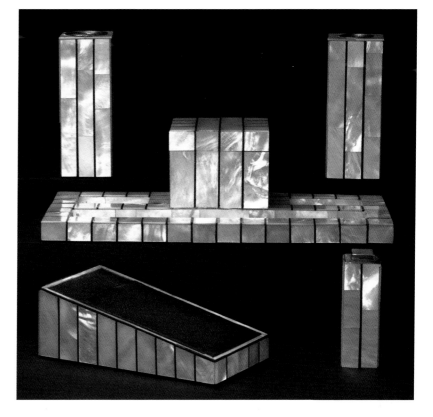

Left page:
Interior of the Wiener Werkstätte sales outlet, Am Graben, Vienna (opened 1907)

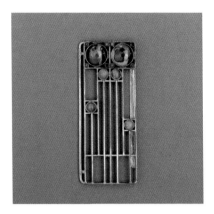

Belt buckle, 1905

Bottom:
Vase, silver, 1904

Above:
Candlesticks, 1903

Left:
Vessel for flowers, hammered silver, 1904

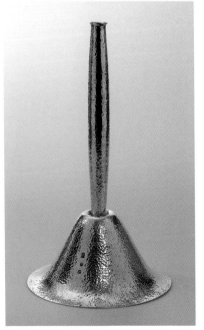

Ashtray, approx. 1906

Right:
Goblet, silver, 1914

Bottom :
Vase, approx. 1905

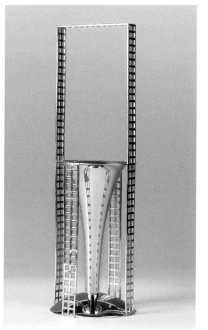

Left:
Coal container, silver, 1905
From the estate of Paul Wittgenstein

Vase, silver, 1909

as "Wiener Werkstätte Productivgenossenschaft von Kunsthandwerkern" (Vienna Workshops of the Production Cooperative of Craft Trade Artisans). The artistic manager was Josef Hoffmann, the commercial manager Koloman Moser. The industrialist Fritz Wärndorfer functioned as the "business associate," meaning financier. The entire adventure, however, was to cost him in the end far more than just the equivalent of the price for a house: in fact all of his wealth.

The goal of the Wiener Werkstätte was to "support the economic interests of its members through training and education in the Arts and Crafts; through the completion of objects from every sector of the crafts trade, based on artistic designs conceived and produced by members of the cooperative; and through the construction of workshops and the sale of the merchandise manufactured." This made it possible to manufacture handicraft products whose artistic and quality standards remained at a consistently high level.

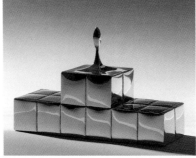

From left to right:
Basket with handle, silver, approx. 1905
Postage stamp moistener, silver, 1905
Eggcup with small spoon, silver, approx. 1904

Bowl, silver, approx. 1919

Coffee service, silver, 1928

The first year of production began with the metal and silver workshop managed in a small apartment in the 4th district of Vienna. At the end of 1903, the firm relocated to the shutdown wing of a factory on Neustiftgasse 32/34. Here Hoffmann and Moser set up exhibition rooms and spaces with drafting tables, together with workshops for carpenters, metalworkers, belt-makers, goldsmiths, bookbinders, varnishers, painters, and makers of leather goods. In addition, located in the uppermost story of a side wing of the factory was the construction office. In its heyday the Wiener Werkstätte employed well over 300 craftspeople.

The working conditions were unusually progressive for that period. The workshops were run according to democratic principles, and the elimination of any intermediate trading entitled the colleagues to a share of the profits. Equally progressive about the setup was the fact that the craftspeople never functioned as anonymous manufacturers; instead, they stood in close contact with the designers and buyers. In this connection, what also qualified as a revolutionary innovation was having the manufactured object initialed by the artist as well as by the participating craftsperson—the artist's monogram appeared in a square, and the craftsperson's in a circle. This promoted a far more

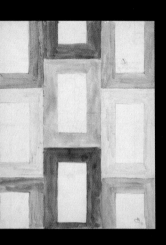
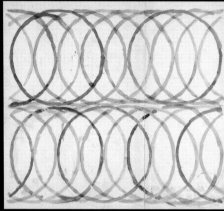

Champagne glass from the "Var. C" drinking service, frosted glass with bronze detailing, design from approx. 1911

Wine glass from the "Var. C" drinking service, frosted glass with bronze detailing, design from approx. 1911

Liqueur glass from the "Var. C" drinking service, frosted glass with bronze detailing, design from approx. 1911

"Redouten" dress (ballroom gown), approx. 1910

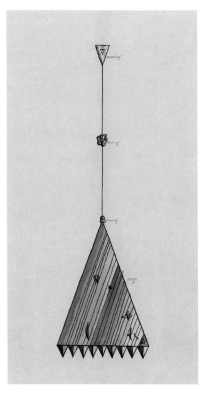
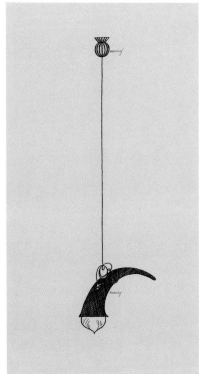
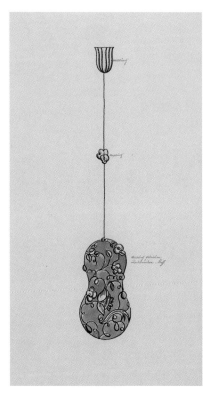

Three lamp designs, between 1925 and 1928

personalized way of identifying the worker with his product. The designs originated from well-known artists such as Gustav Klimt, Oskar Kokoschka, Egon Schiele, Carl Otto Czeschka, Gudrun Baudisch-Wittke, Franz Karl Delavilla, Ernst Lichtblau, Anton Hanak, Mathilde Flögl, Ludwig Heinrich Jungnickel, Anton Kling, Carl Moll, Koloman Moser, Richard Luksch, Dagobert Peche, Emanuel Josef Margold, Michael Powolny, Alfred Roller, Vally Wieselthier, Carl Witzmann, Oskar Strnad—and Josef Hoffmann. The 'all-in-one' nature of the Wiener Werkstätte demanded of workshop artists that they not limit themselves to their own discipline but take part in all the production areas.

This also allowed Hoffmann to present himself as a designer of handcrafted objects and to make a name for himself in this field. In 1910, for example, conductor and composer Gustav Mahler commissioned him to create a tiara for his wife Alma. Hoffmann's catalogue of works lists more than 1000 craft products: furniture, household appliances, book-jacket adornments, jewelry, and fashion items. In the case of these designs as well, Hoffmann consistently varied the initially found forms in a variety of contexts. Some of these objects, such as the latticework basket made of perforated tin plating or silver, rank among the design icons of the twentieth century, attracting top prices at international auctions.

Many of the customers of the Wiener Werkstätte were artists, members of the upper middle class, Jewish high finance and big industry, often represented as well in the Secession environment. Anyway, since the workshops produced only luxury items, the enterprise did not operate cost-efficiently and relied therefore on its supporters. Included among these vital sources were clients from important building projects, people whose spaces Hoffmann designed and outfitted in their entirety as a total work of art, together with his enterprise. In this connection, the Wiener Werkstätte functioned as the 'interior decorating company' for Purkersdorf Sanatorium, Palais Stoclet, Kabarett Fledermaus, and Ast Residence. In addition, from 1907 onward, a workshop outlet designed by Hoffmann in midtown Vienna on Am Graben, No. 15 marketed the products of the Werkstätte. Other outlets were managed at home and abroad: at the famous vacation resorts Karlsbad and Marienbad, Velden on Lake Wörther, as well as in Zurich, Berlin, and overseas in New York.

The first years, between 1903 and 1914, were the most productive. The Wiener Werkstätte was recognized as one of the most interesting and most important enterprises of that period, both in terms of art history and of cultural history. The workshops' products were soon known all throughout Europe, also thanks to the exhibitions that Hoffmann designed at home and abroad: in 1904 at Hohenzollern Arts and Crafts Building in Berlin; in 1905 at Miethke Gallery in Vienna; in 1906 in London, and at Vienna's Kunstschau Exhibition in 1908.

Early on the Wiener Werkstätte experienced a great deal of economic turbulence. In 1914, Wärndorfer, the generous patron of the first years, found himself financially ruined after supporting the workshops and emigrated to the United States. This resulted in the

Bottom left:
Vase with raised base, approx. 1923

Bottom right:
Bowl (from 1915) and jar with lid (after 1918), violet-colored glass with a high polish

Bottom:
Table, black-stained oak timber with white-limed pores, approx. 1903
The grid motif between the table legs serves as bracing.

function of business associate being taken over by Otto Primavesi and his wife Eugenie ("Mäda"), a woman who became known through Gustav Klimt's portrait of her from 1913–1914. Over the years several other financiers tried to save the enterprise. During the inflation years following World War I, a large portion of Vienna's bourgeoisie, which made up the bulk of the regular clientele, lost its assets. This altered the customer profile as much as it did the products: the enterprise increasingly manufactured mass-produced articles—and Adolf Loos promptly scorned what he called the "feminine and eclectic, flea-market Arts and Crafts products of the Wiener Werkstätte."

During the years 1922–1924 the Wiener Werkstätte opened a new branch of its outlets in New York City, on Fifth Avenue, where it unsuccessfully tried to make a fresh start in the New World, in the hope of rescuing its business. Then the final blow came with the Great Depression of 1929 and its consequences: the workshops were liquidated in 1932, and the remaining merchandise put up for public auction. This concluded an important chapter of Austria's cultural history.

Barrel armchair, approx. 1901

Desk from the salon of Dr. Hermann Wittgenstein's apartment, black-stained oak timber, 1905

Left:
Closets for Alfred Roller's apartment, approx. 1906

1904 ▸ Purkersdorf Sanatorium

Wienerstrasse 74, Purkersdorf, Lower Austria

Entrance hall with white-lacquered wooden furniture designed by Hoffmann

Left page:
Exterior view of garden façade

The addition to the 'Westend' Sanatorium in Purkersdorf near Vienna qualifies as more than simply one of the first highlights of Hoffmann's personal, architectural and artistic development; it also represents one of the first situations in which the Wiener Werkstätte's maxims were fully applied. Together with Frank Lloyd Wright's Larkin Building in Buffalo and Otto Wagner's Postal Savings Bank, built in Vienna around the same time, the Purkersdorf Sanatorium is one of the most important constructions of that period.

Josef Hoffmann received the commission from sanatorium director Viktor Zuckerkandl. He was recommended for the job by the director's sister-in-law, Bertha Zuckerkandl, a journalist and art critic and one of the most important people associated with the Secession. She supported contemporary artists such as Gustav Klimt

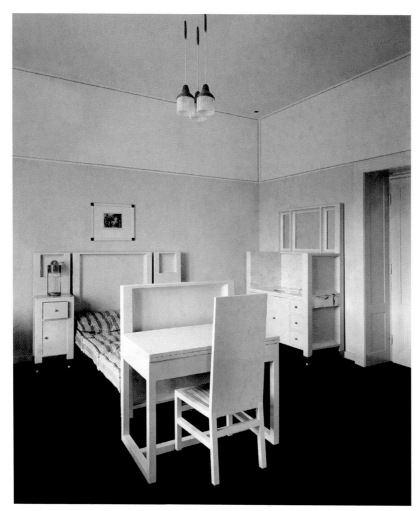

and Egon Schiele and wrote comprehensive texts about Hoffmann's architecture. In 1916 she commissioned him with the furnishing of her private apartment.

This assignment was as new as it was unconventional: constructing a sanatorium, with health spas and areas for administering physical therapy and treating nervous disorders, which simultaneously offered its wealthy clientele the corresponding comfort and luxury. This architectural task gave Hoffmann the chance to combine the architecture and furnishings into a total work of art in keeping with the ideals of the Wiener Werkstätte. Aided by what was considered then a modern building material, reinforced concrete, he also had the opportunity to establish a vital relationship between construction, function, and form.

The design of the building is based on a square, which assumes here the character of a leitmotif—apparent in the floor tiles' black-and-white quadratic pattern, the use of quadratic basic forms for the exposed concrete joists of the walls and ceilings, and in the design of the windows and doors. Even the ground plan of the ground floor level is composed of two squares. The strict axial and symmetrical form of the structure is intensified by the square-shaped windows and tiles.

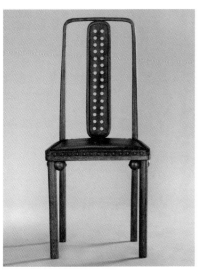

The treatment and utility rooms were located on the ground floor and raised ground-floor levels. Social rooms, entertainment areas, and a large dining hall were on the first story, while the second story accommodated guestrooms. The interiors were designed entirely by the Wiener Werkstätte, their spaces and inventory carefully coordinated one with the other. The first story was given green tones, and a wealth of hanging lamps as well as wall lighting fittings, creating both a modern and extensive lighting situation. The new building was connected to the existing construction by a pump room made of wood and glass.

With Purkersdorf Sanatorium, Hoffmann succeeded in laying down the basic design principles of modernism. Following its deterioration and subsequent renovation, the building could meanwhile be reconstructed.

1905–1906 ▸ Beer-Hofmann Residence

Hasenauerstrasse 59 at the corner of Meridianplatz, Vienna XVIII

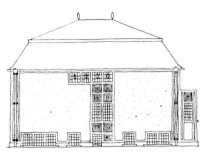

Perspective of west façade

The poet Richard Beer-Hofmann belonged to Vienna's late Romantic period. In his works he strived for a revival of awareness of life based on legend. Josef Hoffmann met the poet through the circle of friends associated with Vienna Secession. According to one Viennese anecdote, Hoffmann came up with the design for Beer-Hofmann's house in a café, in the early hours of the morning, following a soirée in Max Reinhardt's chambers at the Hotel Imperial, where client and architect, together with assorted friends, spent a long and intimate night together.

The construction period lasted eleven months. The building costs were documented as being exactly 133,712 Austrian crowns. To better understand the value of this sum, it helps to compare it to the yearly salary of a public schoolteacher at that time, around 1,200 crowns—or to what had been the price of a large portrait by the famous Secessionist painter Gustav Klimt, around 10,000 crowns.

With its approximately 717 square yards of floor area, spacious social rooms, and 16.4-foot-high hall, this large building clearly refers to the cultured lifestyle of the bourgeois intellectual. Besides a music room, it featured a smoking room, library, and dining room area. All the L-shaped rooms were arranged about the hall and created a lengthy sequence of spaces offering a variety of atmospheres and functions.

The ground plan of this building with a classical façade demonstrates a thoroughly modern attitude. The architectural innovation involved here showed itself also in the interior of the house: the spacious English living hall with fireplace was given the type of black-and-white checkerboard floor pattern typical of a Hoffmann design. Superimposing this Viennese Art Nouveau style design on the English-style hall typology leads to a visual excitement of its own.

In Beer-Hofmann's house the elite from the worlds of theater and literature often came together for informal evenings, though never for large-scale soirées. Among the poet's regular guests were Peter Altenberg, Raoul Aslan, Hermann Bahr, Tina Blau, Hugo von Hoffmannsthal, Thomas Mann, Max Reinhardt, Rainer Maria Rilke, Alfred Roller, Arthur Schnitzler, Richard Strauss, Franz Werfel, and Bertha Zuckerkandl.

Richard Beer-Hofmann, forced to flee from Austria in 1939, died in exile in New York in 1945. Since there was apparently no interest on the part of the rightful heirs to preserve the building, it was, after decades of neglect, in a desolate state. Unfortunately, Josef Hoffmann's remarkable creation was finally torn down in 1970, and even today the plot remains unused.

Left page:
Street view, approx. 1906

Left:
Woman's bedroom with large bay window facing south

Right page:
View of the poet's study

Bottom:
Upper section of hall with stairway to attic floor

1905–1911 ▸ Palais Stoclet
Tervurenlaan 281, Brussels, Belgium

Left page:
Roof terrace over garage entrance with stair turret

Right:
Overall view from the street

The Palais Stoclet in Brussels ranks among the most important residential buildings of the twentieth century. Widely considered a milestone of modern architecture, it represents the most significant total work of art created through the efforts of the Wiener Werkstätte: the building's overall construction, interior architecture, and garden architecture were combined here to form a harmonic whole. Simultaneously the building made manifest the congenial collaboration between architect and client.

Adolphe Stoclet, the heir to a Belgian financial empire, married Suzanne Stevens, the daughter of the well-known Paris-based art dealer Arthur Stevens. After living in Milan, the young art-loving couple moved to Vienna, soon becoming associated with the environment of the Secession. Originally, it was planned that Hoffmann would build a house for the Stoclet family on a property later used for the Ast Residence. But when the death of Stoclet's father forced him to return to Brussels in order to come into his paternal inheritance, Hoffmann was commissioned to meet the plan in Brussels.

Although Hoffmann began the designing of the construction in 1905, and gained permission to begin building on July 29, 1906, another five years were needed to complete the three-story 'Palais'. The building's exterior is surfaced entirely with white slabs of Norwegian Turili marble. All the essential, structure-giving surfaces and windows are edged with black-oxidized copper profiles, each adorned with intricately embossed gilded ornaments. Rising from a approximately 31.5-foot-high main building is an almost 65.6-foot-high cubical stepped tower at the top of which stand four figures. The ground plan, which measures roughly 121 by 43 feet, is provided with two main axes running at right angles to one another. The building's structural presence refers to the traditional English country house. It features a spacious two-story hall,

View into the two-story hall

Right:
Ground plan of first floor

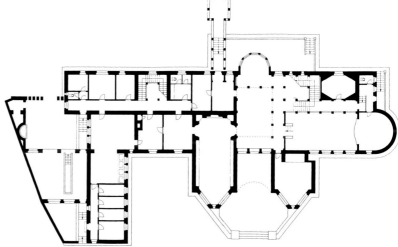

reception rooms on the ground floor, private bedrooms on the first story, and additional rooms for guests and servants in the loft conversion.

However, the true wealth of Hoffmann's directorial artistry unfolds in the building's interior. This is where an astounding spatial artwork was created in collaboration with Wiener Werkstätte artists such as Kolo Moser, Gustav Klimt, Michael Powolny, and Carl Otto Czeschka. Regarding the detail work, each room contains a surprise of its own: the vestibule's walls are surfaced with Verde-antico marble; the floors are made of white marble; and the two-story hall, which rises to a height of 23.62 feet and stands illuminated from two sides, has pillars and walls surfaced with Paonazzo and Belgian marble, flooring made of inlayed dark wood, and chamois leather upholstered furniture. Forming a strong contrast to these details is the music and theater room's dark-hued floor made of teak and coral wood, its walls surfaced with polished, black-toned Portovenere marble and accented by gilded copper mouldings, and the red furniture with matching red curtains. The highlight on the ground floor is no doubt the extravagant and spacious dining room area with wall mosaics by

Top right:
Breakfast room

Top left:
Dining room
The wall surfacing is made of Paonazzo marble
and decorated with mosaics by Gustav Klimt.

Kitchen

Left:
Detail of Gustav Klimt's wall mosaic

Top left:
Daughters' room

Top right:
Woman's dressing room

Parents' bathroom

Left:
**Children's room with animal friezes by Ludwig
H. Jungnickel**

Gustav Klimt—*Die Erwartung* (Expectation) depicting a dancer, and *Die Erfüllung* (Fulfillment) depicting two lovers. Offsetting the formal and almost courtly atmosphere of the dining room is the cheerful, wall surface chosen for the breakfast room, boasting a floral pattern based on the colors yellow and white.

The sensual opulence is continued in the private bedrooms and bathrooms—via the marble staircase leading to the upper level of the hall. The master bedroom is surfaced with polished Palisander wood. The bordering bathroom, with a floor area measuring 19.7 by 19 feet, is determined by a large bathtub made of white marble; its walls are surfaced with pale statuary marble, while the floor is tiled with dark-blue Belge marble. The complete bathroom furnishings, including all the silver utensils, were custom-made by the Wiener Werkstätte.

When art historian Karl Ernst Osthaus, founder of the Folkwang Museum in Hagen, learned of the completion of the Palais, he interrupted the board meeting of the German Werkbund in session at that moment and announced: "The owner of the Palais Stoclet in Brussels has just moved into his new accommodations—a work whose spiritual depth and artistic dignity has not been seen in Europe since the Baroque period." Jean Cocteau, Anatole France, Sacha Guitry, and Igor Strawinsky were among the many personalities and artists to visit this remarkable structure and sign the silver-plated guest book designed by Hoffmann. With this building, Hoffmann not only helped to elevate the splendor of that period to an authentic spatial expression; he also reached the zenith of his architectural output.

Following a dispute among the heirs, it could be legally guaranteed that the building and its inventory would remain protected as a total work of art. Now too, the 'Palais' is to be entered in the UNESCO World Heritage List.

1906 ‣ Hunting Lodge for Karl Wittgenstein
Hochreith near Hohenberg, Lower Austria

Living room with wooden paneling made of precious Maracaibo wood.
On the right a chest of drawers with mirrors.

The results of this commissioned work fascinate to the same degree as the biography of its client, Karl Wittgenstein, brother of Paul Wittgenstein and father of the famous philosopher Ludwig Wittgenstein. He was an exceptional patron of Vienna Secession and Wiener Werkstätte, without whose support the Vienna Secession Building by Joseph Maria Olbrich would have probably never existed. The architectural task at hand was to rebuild two rooms of Karl Wittgenstein's hunting lodge. The altered spaces had to reflect the client's social status and aristocratic lifestyle, while satisfying the representative demands of a steel industry magnate at the same time.

Living room
The room can be divided by a curtain. A chest of drawers with mirrors is visible on the left and a playing table on the right.

Anteroom
Decorative painting by Czeschka and Hoffmann, ceramics by Luksch

Karl Wittgenstein was the son of a wealthy wool dealer. Strong-willed and highly gifted, he left home at the age of seventeen after being expelled from high school for challenging the immortality of the soul in an essay. With a violin packed in his luggage, he spent two years wandering the United States and held various jobs on the road. He worked as a bar musician and waiter, gave violin and horn lessons, and taught Latin, Greek, math, and music. After returning to Austria and studying briefly at the Technical University of Vienna, he began the breathtaking career which, within two decades, turned him into one of Europe's wealthiest men, an "Austrian Krupp," and the embodiment of the successful industrial magnate: in 1877, at the age of thirty, he was already director of the Teplitz rolling mill, and a few years later its principal stockholder. After taking over Prague's company for steel production, the Prager Eisenindustriegesellschaft, he founded Austria's first iron industrial cartel, purchased the St. Aegyd Ironworks and, in 1897, reached the height of his influence by buying up the majority of the shares of the Austrian-Alpine Construction Company. The following year, at the ripe old age of fifty-one, he retired from the world of business and devoted himself to his two passions: hunting and art.

For today's viewer these spaces seem to create a wonderland manufactured by the Wiener Werkstätte. The grand salon, measuring 15.1 by 21.3 feet and surfaced with waffled Marakaibo wood paneling, is given gilded framing profiles. The built-in furniture is of the highest quality. The entire anteroom was designed by artists of the Wiener Werkstätte, with paintings by Carl Otto Czeschka, ceramics by Richard Luksch, and decorative glasswork, most likely by Kolo Moser.

1906–1907 · Hochstetter House
Steinfeldgasse 7, Vienna XIX

Street view

Left page:
Garden view

Kitchen with the black-and-white square floor tiles characteristic of Hoffmann's designs

Helene Hochstetter was the sister-in-law of Paul Wittgenstein, director of the St. Aegyd Ironworks. In 1901–1902 Hoffmann had already furnished an apartment for her in Vienna. In 1914 Helene Hochstetter was also mentioned as one of the Wiener Werkstätte's associates.

In 1906 Hoffmann's client purchased a piece of property that offered a view of the City of Vienna. This was located on Steinfeldgasse, diagonally facing the Moser-Moll double house. In May and June of the same year, the submitted building plans were approved, and about a year later the house was completed. Parallel to working on Hochstetter's house, Hoffmann worked on Adolphe Stoclet's Palais. Although the building for Hochstetter is infinitely more modest than the Palais in Brussels, one can compare the half-rounded bay window to its counterpart in the building for Stoclet and point to other shared architectural details, such as wall niches given rhythm by pillar arrangements.

The façade design could be thought uncommon for Vienna, because the entire ground floor is surfaced with exposed light-colored clinker brick, while the upper story is given the usual grainy coat of plaster. Particularly the designs for Hochstetter's house, published in the magazine *Der Architekt*, show a strong affinity to architectural designs by Charles Rennie Mackintosh. Especially characteristic here is the covered entranceway loggia, leading from the sidewalk to the entrance door, revealing here yet another element of Hochstetter's house reminiscent of the Palais Stoclet in Brussels.

The interior design perfectly corresponds with the client's many social obligations: located on the ground floor are the main hall, grand living room, and dining room; the basement-level kitchen is reached via a separate stairway. The bedrooms and a guestroom on the upper floor are accessed via a main staircase, which develops from the hall. Here the building indicates a separation of social functions typical of an upper middle-class home: the public-familial stairwell on the one side, and the service stairs for servants on the other.

After minor damage inflicted during World War II, the building was, beginning from 1960, extensively rebuilt and heightened, becoming a hotel-pension. In the process its special architectural qualities were systematically destroyed, and later the building was torn down. Today the property is occupied by a large multifamily building.

1907 ‣ Kabarett Fledermaus
Kärntnerstrasse 33 at the corner of Johannesgasse 1, Vienna I

The entry with the bar

Design anteroom for Kabarett Fledermaus

On October 20, 1907, the Wiener Werkstätte opened their famous avant-garde cabaret and theater-bar named "Die Fledermaus" (The Bat). The cultural historian Egon Friedell described the situation as follows: "In 1907, Fritz Wärndorfer, a cultivated man with a great deal of money and taste—two things we all know rarely come together— came up with the idea of creating a cabaret ... in collaboration with the Wiener Werkstätte. Everything from the bar counter's bright tiles to the theater hall, fashioned entirely in black-and-white tones, was a spellbinding treasure of intimacy and high-mindedness. Consequently, all of Vienna ... used to receiving red velvet and gilded plaster surfaces for its money ... went perfectly wild over it. The opening night ended in tremendous uproar."

In November 1907, when Charles Édouard Jeanneret—later known as Le Corbusier —came to Vienna to study the latest developments in the fields of architecture and design, he was so impressed by the interior of this cavernous nightspot that he captured it in a carefully rendered drawing.

There was no denying that Josef Hoffmann and his artist-colleagues of the Wiener Werkstätte, Bertold Löffler, Michael Powolny, Gustav Klimt, Oskar Kokoschka, and others, succeeded in creating a design sensation with the furnishings for the cabaret— an establishment spread over the 526.24 square yards in the basement of a newly constructed building. After descending the staircase, visitors were first received in an

Two-story auditorium

The famous "Fledermaus Chair"

anteroom with bar, whose mind-boggling brightness was only known until then in paintings by Klimt. The randomly sized, ornamental tiles and depictions of figures on the walls gave visitors the impression they were entering a never suspected counter-world of the wildest imaginings. What followed, as a contrast, were the cabaret's hall and stage, dominated by an unadorned black-and-white. The gallery offered eight box seats. In the auditorium tables and chairs were arranged on carpeting with a black-and-white pattern. In this way, Hoffmann had also managed to create a total work of art of a different order: since the cabaret's interior coordinated the silverware, lighting elements, stage decorations, posters, postcards, entrance tickets, and printed menus one with another, he simultaneously created a corporate identity—in the same year that Peter Behrens was commissioned to carry out a similar task, even though on a much larger scale, for AEG (General Electricity Company) in Berlin.

The architectural sensation was given two finishing touches: the barman came from the United States, and the master chef from Paris. Among the performing artists to regularly appeared onstage were the Wiesenthal sisters, Gertrude Barrison, Marya Delvard, Peter Altenberg (as an MC), Alfred Polgar, and Egon Friedell, the cabaret's artistic director in the years 1908–1909.

Only six years later the 'Fledermaus' was forced to shut down, after which the cabaret was rebuilt so many times that its original layout vanished.

1909–1911 ▸ Ast Residence
Steinfeldgasse 2 / Wollergasse 12, Vienna XIX

Street view

The wealthy, building contractor Eduard Ast, who pioneered Austria's reinforced concrete industry and was a patron of the Vienna Secession's artists and the Wiener Werkstätte, had often collaborated with Hoffmann in the capacity of contractor. During the period when Hoffmann was completing Palais Stoclet in Brussels, he received from Ast a commission that gave him the opportunity to create another luxury building.

Completed in an amazingly short amount of time (between May 1910 and March 1911), Ast Residence was the last building erected as a structural component of the "Hohe Warte Artists' Colony". It was bordered by properties on which two others buildings designed by Hoffmann stood: to one side Friedrich Spitzer's residence, built ten years earlier, which, in juxtaposition with Eduard Ast's villa, made evident the development of Hoffmann's formal language; to the other side Moll's house No. 2, built in 1906–1907, the second house of the stepfather and the mother of Alma Mahler-Werfel.

Viewed from the street, the villa seems monumental because the main story stands on a foundation structure made of dry rubble. The elevated garden is arranged around a pond with decoratively curved edges. At the west end of the house a glazed loggia is continued through the garden as a five-axial covered walkway. Regarding the façade design, a special request expressed by the building contractor plays a major role: it was required that the incrustation technique, which Ast himself perfected, be carried out in an exemplary fashion on all the cornices, façade surfaces and window profiles, as well as on the decorative cornices and façade ornaments. During this phase of Hoffmann's creative output, his marked interest in neoclassicism is reflected in the pilaster-like and vertically emphasized rigidity of the façades' cabled fluting.

No differently than during the construction of Palais Stoclet, for this project too, money was no object. The reception rooms were both of the highest quality and color-coordinated: The living hall was surfaced with Laaser marble; the dining room with brownish-black, orange, and white-veined Portovenere marble; and the oval salon given a grayish-green Cipollion marble (often also used by Adolf Loos), with a color contrast established here by hanging Gustav Klimt's painting *Danae* at the spatial axis.

Ast's businesses suffered such bitter losses during the Depression that he was forced to sell his residence in 1931. Apart from that, the building was laden with an aura of doom: this was after all where he lost two of his children. The next person to own it was Alma Mahler-Werfel, and for a good six years Ast Residence served as the stage for the social circle of an intriguing and famous woman, a woman as controversial as surrounded by scandal—at first the wife of Gustav Mahler, Alma married the architect Walter Gropius, following a passionate affair with the painter Oskar Kokoschka, and finally married the writer Franz Werfel. But it was in this house that Manon Gropius, Alma's daughter with Gropius, died in 1935 at the age of nineteen. Later, Alban Berg would dedicate his concert for violin and orchestra to the young woman—a work he entitled *Dem Andenken eines Engels* (In Memory of an Angel). "I blame everything on this house, on this accursed house," wrote Alma in her diary.

Left page:
Garden view with decorative pond

West-facing garden façade with
characteristic fluting

Right:
Lamps

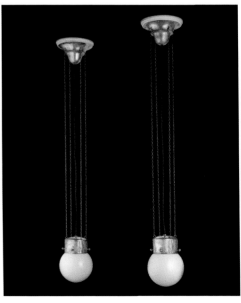

Living hall with view into oval salon (right)

In June of 1937—the *Anschluss* of Austria by Germany already deteriorating—Alma and Franz Werfel threw a bacchanalian farewell party for more than 160 invited guests, among which where representatives from the worlds of big business, industry, and politics, and artists such as Alexander von Zemlinsky, Bruno Walter, Ida Roland, Carl Zuckmayer, Ödön von Horváth, and Franz Theodor Csokor. The party was obviously a huge success: it lasted well into the afternoon of the following day. During the course of the festivities, Werfel collapsed drunk into the villa's ornamental pond, and Zuckmayer ended up sleeping in the dog kennel.

The following year the majority of the invited artists and their hosts were in exile. Today, with its interior greatly altered, Ast Residence functions as an ambassadorial residence.

1913–1915 · Skywa-Primavesi Residence

Gloriettegasse 18, Vienna XIII

Left page:
Street façade

Right:
Garden façade

Entrance hall with staircase

It was the banker Otto Primavesi, one of the financiers for the Wiener Werkstätte, who recommended Hoffmann to the client, the banker's cousin Robert. Robert Primavesi was well-acquainted with the notion of representation: He was a parliamentarian, the owner of great amounts of property, and a major industrialist who enjoyed spending time at his hunting lodge in Moravia, where he sometimes organized weekend outings for as many as fifty guests. It would be more appropriate to call his city residence in Wien-Hietzing a "palace," comparable to Palais Stoclet in Brussels. Robert Primavesi and his companion Josefine Skywa ran it as a center for the Viennese high society.

The building's neoclassical rigidity recalls Hoffmann's Austrian House, shown at the German Werkbund Exhibition in Cologne in 1914. This enormous structure with over 1,196 square yards for its living spaces and auxiliary structures was built in an exclusive setting—on a site offering 5,142.7 square yards of floor area in the refined suburb of Vienna known as Hietzing, and in the immediate vicinity of Schönbrunn Castle. The submitted building plans are dated in May 1913, and the legal documents approving the building's use by the owners were signed in January 1915.

Architecturally Hoffmann organized the construction around a centralized two-story hall given an ornamented wall paneling. Facing the street it showcases an eleven-axial and 98.4-foot-long façade featuring two pediment-crowned lateral projections: a work of neoclassical architecture, which, on the strength of its finely subdivided and fluted pillars, has an almost Art Deco-like quality. The official character of the villa's façade facing the street is strengthened by two gable-inserted figures by the artist Anton Hanak, one of the most important sculptors of that period. The stringent

Large dining room
The furniture was designed by Hoffmann

architecture of the villa's garden-facing façade is greatly subdivided by bay windows, sun lounges, and recesses, making it almost possible to speak of an "official" and a "private" façade. In spite of this powerful structural differentiation, the residence nevertheless emits great peace.

The monumental design of the main entrance with a porte cochère or carriage gate and grandly scaled staircase in the entrance hall reflects the owner's special wish for representation. The outfitting of the villa's interior is of a consistently high quality. Not only does the paneled hall generate a sophisticated and elegant aura; the same can be said of the salon's lemon wood floor with inlayed black strips and its Arabescato marble used for the baseboards and doorway framing. Yet the owner's study, whose walls were lined with Oriental carpets, could only be called unusually eccentric.

The representative aura is consistently extended into the garden design. Here the luxuriousness of the city villa is completed by a small teahouse with pergola and a spacious greenhouse decked with a barrel-shaped glass roof.

1924·The Ast Country House

Auen-Waldpromenade 35–36, Aue near Velden on Lake Wörther, Carinthia

First design of the Ast Residence

After years of successful collaborations with building contractor Eduard Ast, and having already built his residence on Hohe Warte in Vienna (1909–1911), fifteen years later Hoffmann was commissioned to build for the contractor a well-proportioned vacation house at the famous holiday resort Velden on Lake Wörther. The expansive, sloped property offers an excellent view of the lake and surrounding mountains. Lake Wörther's Mediterranean flair evolves from the mildness of the region's summer climate and its nearness to Italy. Many stately, turn-of-the-century summer residences are located at different points around the lake.

The gardens, gatehouse, and main house are connected by a coordinating spatial sequence. Executed as a dry rubble construction, the carriage house clearly distinguishes itself from the elegant two-story vacation house with its horizontal profiling and bright-colored plaster coat. The house and its living spaces develop to the south and not to the north, towards the lake.

A novelty is the rhythmically designed, horizontal orientation of the façade and the flat roof, produced here by the classical box-type windows. Here too, Hoffmann's architectural language comes that much closer to reflecting the influence of current devel-

Overall view shortly after completion

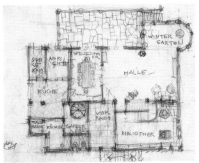

First sketch of the ground-floor plan

opments in international architecture. The façades' horizontal plaster ornaments and flat roof lend the house a modern appearance. Just the same, compared to villas designed by Le Corbusier around this time, Ast's Country House seems less radical and more like an expression of middle-class cheerfulness.

The division of the interior spaces is functional. A staircase leads from the living hall to the first upper story, which houses bedrooms and guestrooms. The main staircase leads to the second story, where a four-sided glazed observation tower offers both a commanding view of the landscape and access to the roof terrace.

Modern in an moderate manner, while demonstrating an enormous sympathy for the wishes of its user the color-coordinated spaces and furniture of the country house reflect the full range of qualities found in Hoffmann's spatial art.

1923–1925▸Housing Complex Klosehof
Philippovichgasse 1, Vienna XIX

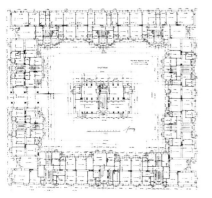

Ground plan of ground floor

In the years following World War I Vienna's governing social democratic party launched a social housing development scheme meant to remedy the city's raging housing shortage. Primarily, the project was financed by Vienna's housing development tax and the profits gained from rent takings. Until 1934, approximately 65,000 public-assisted dwelling units were built in Vienna.

Josef Hoffmann was among the first architects to receive a commission from the City of Vienna for the construction of a housing estate. In the fall of 1923, he was entrusted with the planning of "Klosehof," a housing facility containing 140 apartments and located in the refined Wien-Döbling area, to which the Hohe Warte Artists' Colony also belonged. Politically, the goal of this measure was to alter the population structure of a district formerly inhabited solely by middle-class citizens. Situated in this district as well was the more than half-a-mile-long apartment block "Karl-Marx-Hof," also called "Ringstrasse des Proletariats" (The Proletarian's Ring Road), designed by Karl Ehn and constructed in the years 1927–1930.

For his plan, Hoffmann had at his disposal an entire almost-square block of building property with approximately 197-foot-long sides. He developed the five-story block with ten stairwells and placed a six-story residential tower in the middle of the site, where he included ground-floor areas for children and four small apartments per story.

The entire housing complex was designed as a simple, plastered structure. Originally, its surfaces were to be offset by window frames painted red and protruding somewhat out of line with the plastering. Remarkable about the housing complex is its tower, positioned in the interior of the court development—a building part originally

Right:
Courtyard entrance

Left page:
Entrance with the sculptures "Früchteträger-innen" (Women Carrying Trays of Fruit) by Anton Hanak

Left:
Interior courtyard
The courtyard façades' projections are crowned by triangular pediments.

Right page:
Apartment tower at the interior courtyard

Children's recreational facilities in apartment tower

intended to rise even higher. The restrained design with its laterally arranged pairs of three-sectioned casement windows and centralized pairs of circular windows gives the structure a monumentality akin to neo-objectivity. When studied in vintage black-and-white photographs, this architecture seems to anticipate Ludwig Hilberseimer's metropolitan architecture.

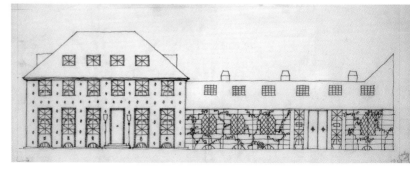

1924–1925·Sonja Knips Residence
Nusswaldgasse 22, Vienna XIX

Left page, top:
Street view

Left page, bottom:
Drawing of façade with auxiliary building

Around the time Hoffmann was completing Ast's Country House on Lake Wörther, he began designing a townhouse for Sonja Knips. This was in fact the last city villa that Hoffmann ever built, and no differently than this type of construction, his client too belonged to a meanwhile extinct world.

Sophie Amalia Maria Knips, called Sonja Knips and née Baroness Potier des Echelles, is best known through Klimt's marvelous painting of her from 1898, the artist's first modern portrait of a woman, depicting Sonja as a young and beautiful subject aged twenty-five. Married to the industrialist Anton Knips, owner of an iron factory in Bohemia, she belonged to the circle of important sponsors of the Wiener Werkstätte, and her sense of commitment greatly surpassed the mere collection of the workshops' creations.

Josef Hoffmann could have been called a close friend of the family. As early as 1903, he furnished the Knips family's town flat on Gumpendorferstrasse, and he oversaw as well the expansion and remodeling of the same apartment in 1915–1916. He designed not only their summerhouse on Lake Millstätter in the Carinthia region (1903), but also the family's burial site in the Wien-Hietzing Cemetery (1919). Sonja Knips purchased the property for the city villa on Nusswaldgasse 22 from journalist Bertha Zuckerkandl. She was so impressed by the collaboration with Hoffmann that, soon after its completion, she considered selling the building in order to have the pleasure of collaborating with him again on another project.

With regard to the distribution of the constructional volume, the Knips residence respects the type of English country house architecture oriented towards the Arts and Crafts movement: it offers a main house with a lateral, structural addition for auxiliary spaces. The asymmetrical structure divulges an almost objectifying interpretation of the façade with equally distributed windows with an upright format and an approximately 8 inches framing on the ground floor, which causes them to jut forward and out of line with the façade, structured by small rhomboidal pargetings. The hipped roof recalls Viennese Biedermeier style to which the immediate surroundings are structurally obliged for the most part.

Dining room

The distribution of the interior space as well indicates a functionality akin to neo-objectivity. The living hall optically connects to the dining room by way of wall-high glass doors, similar to what happens with kitchen and pantry. The interior was realized by the Wiener Werkstätte, partly utilizing furniture taken from the town apartment on Gumpendorferstrasse. The ornamentations are by Christine Ehrlich and Michael Powolny, and the furniture's upholstery was completed using designs by Dagobert Peche. The house boasted three important paintings by Gustav Klimt: *Obstbäume* (Fruit Trees), hanging in the dining room, *Adam and Eve* in the female room, and the portrait of *Sonja Knips* decorated the library on the upper story.

The owner of the house died in 1959. Fortunately, up into the present, the building was never subjected to large-scale structural interventions.

1928–1932 › Housing Complex Laxenburgerstrasse

Laxenburgerstrasse 94, Vienna X

This housing complex was planned during the years of the Great Depression in 1928–1929, and permission to use its spaces granted in February 1933—a year before the social housing program was cancelled by order of the Austro-fascist corporative state.

In December 1930, when Hoffmann celebrated his sixtieth birthday, the numerous tributes paid to him came from colleagues at home and abroad, and not least of all from representatives of the avant-garde of the Modern. To the same extent his works were already recognized as historical, Hoffmann's understanding of architecture and arts and crafts (in the spirit of William Morris) as a revolutionary act, had become history. Thus, his works no longer belonged to the avant-garde.

The proportions of this five-story construction on Laxenburgerstrasse were monumental: 249.3 feet wide and nearly 406.8 feet long. Hoffmann's design favors a rather uniform handling of the façade, in which for the most part larger open surfaces are subdivided by balconies. With 16 stairwells, the 332 apartments are primarily developed in groups of four. Only the stairwells in the four corners of the complex develop apartments in groups of six. The spacious inner courtyard with greenery functions as a

View from the corner of Dieselgasse and Leebgasse

recreational area in an otherwise densely built-up city district. Unlike other housing complexes with inner courtyards and built at the same time as this one in Vienna's inner city, Hoffmann's works demonstrate a both reduced objectivity and the type of staged, optical presence first taken up again following World War II. With regard to the social housing scheme, Josef Hoffmann defended an architectural standpoint similar to that of his colleagues Josef Frank and Ernst Lichtblau: instead of living as a form of

View from Reichenbachgasse

presentation, living was now to be understood as a reduction to functional aspects, such as natural lighting, allusion to exterior spaces, and rationally conceived ground plans—at best, these social housing dwelling units would allow itself to be seen as unspectacular, and taken for granted as an expression of 'natural dignity'.

In 1983, the housing complex was christened "Anton Hölzl Courts" in memory of the national assembly member and cofounder of the Non-Political Workers Federation.

1930–1932 ▸ Row Houses at Werkbund Exhibition

Veitingergasse 79–85, Vienna XIII

View of street façade with the staircase towers

Josef Hoffmann was a founding member of the Austrian Werkbund, an association of Austrian architects, designers, and industrialists, in which he served as a member of the board in 1914 and in 1928. He participated in many Werkbund's exhibitions, including the exhibition in Vienna held in 1930, dedicated to the idea of the "New Building".

In the same year, under the direction of Josef Frank, the Werkbund began with the construction of a pilot scheme housing settlement—a project modeled after the Weissenhof settlement in Stuttgart, realized in the course of the exhibition of the German Werkbund in 1927. The Viennese exhibition opened on June 4, 1932. But unlike the Stuttgart exhibition it only proved significant on a local level. Moreover, the names

Garden view, 1932

of leading representatives of the New Building such as Le Corbusier, Walter Gropius, and Mies van der Rohe were missing. Apart from Hoffmann, the other architects to participate in the housing settlement's construction were André Lurçat, Gerritt Rietveld, Adolf Loos, Ernst Plischke, Hugo Häring, and Ernst Lichtblau. Altogether seventy new buildings were completed.

Hoffmann's contribution to the Werkbund's exhibition was a set of four row houses erected on Veitingergasse. Based on two different types of ground plans, they mirrored one another according to the juxtapositioning of the central buildings and the corner houses. The larger building type (the corner houses) contained with its floor space of approximately 904 square feet one room more than the smaller variation of

Living room with view into bedroom

Bottom:
Entrance with glazed staircase tower

710.4 square feet of floor space. The buildings had a north-to-south orientation with living spaces and terraces directed toward a garden facing south.

Notable here are the totally glazed stairwells which rise up over the single-story structure and develop a roof terrace. The undecorated, smooth façade with single windows is designed to interact with a glazed stair turret, which in turn contributes to breaking up the monotony of the row houses. One could even argue that this suggested aspect of movement is a metaphor for the Modern.

Built using conventional construction methods with plastered timber brick walls, the structure fails to convey the experimental character attributed to avant-garde architecture, yet it does embody a tangible modernism. The roof terrace welcomes associations with projects by Le Corbusier and conveys a hint of Mediterranean exoticism to Vienna.

Above:
Drawing of the façade
View from Veitingergasse

Bottom:
Ground plan sketch

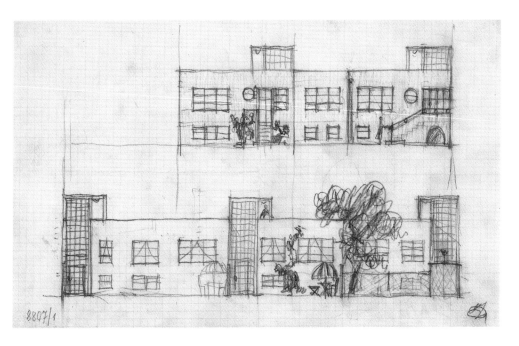

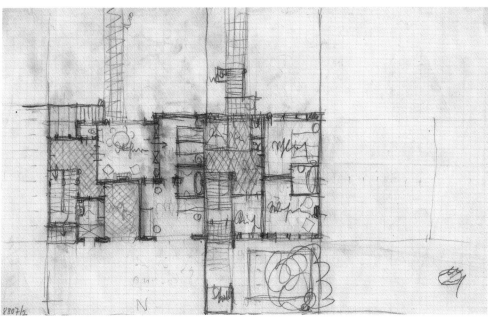

1934·Austrian Pavilion at Venice Biennale
Venice, Italy

Exhibition hall

Left page:
View of the front side with entrance portal

With the Austrian Pavilion created for the 1934 Venice Biennale Josef Hoffmann produced his last internationally significant work of architecture—a project realized in conjunction with a competition limited to only six architects: Erich Boltenstern, Joseph Dex, Eugen Kastner, Robert Kramreiter, Hermann Kutschera and Josef Hoffmann. Hoffmann, who emerged the winner, erected the pavilion together with Oswald Haerdtl, his office partner at that time. Robert Kramreiter oversaw the construction services. The opening of the still incomplete pavilion took place on May 12, 1934. Hoffmann was not present for the opening ceremony and later complained of unauthorized changes being made on the pavilion.

Hoffmann created a simple, rectangular structure with two low-rise, short and laterally-recessed wing additions which spread out from the rear of the structure to form a small courtyard. The shape of the overall ground plan suggests a wide 'U'. The entire pavilion is elevated on a stone-paved terrace foundation. In the middle, a large portal the height of the structure affords a view into the courtyard with a fountain surrounded by a water basin. The portal is surfaced with slabs of Travertine, and the plaster surfacing of the façade is horizontally striated. Due to financial difficulties and the lack of time, Hoffmann had to do without the ornaments and sculptures meant to enhance the pavilion's portal and entranceway. Instead, all that appeared was the word "Austria" spelled out in delicate letters on the surface of the left wall.

The pavilion has four exhibition spaces. Both of the large main rooms are illuminated by ribbon windows directly below the flat ceiling, redirecting the light for the suspended illuminating glass ceiling. In the main rooms, the ceiling height is 22.3 feet (18 feet from floor to glass ceiling), and in the side rooms somewhat higher than 13.1 feet.

Following Austria's *Anschluss* by Germany in 1938, the pavilion remained unused until 1948. After World War II, Hoffmann remained the Biennale's commissioner from 1948 to his death in 1956. During this period he enhanced the pavilion with small, structural additions. In 1984—for its 50th anniversary—the pavilion's original design was meticulously restored by architect Hans Hollein, also the Biennale's commissioner at that time.

Ground plan

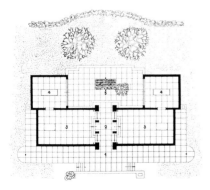

Life and Work

Note: The numerous furnishings for private apartments and outlets of Wiener Werkstätte, the gravestone designs, individual articles designed for interiors, as well as projects that were not executed, are not included in the following list of works.

1870 ▶ Josef Franz Maria Hoffmann is born December 15 in Pirnitz (Brtnice) near Iglau, in Moravia (today the Czech Republic). His father is Josef Franz Karl Hoffmann, the town's mayor and co-owner of the cotton production plant of Prince Collalto's textile firm, and his mother Leopoldine Hoffmann, née Tuppy.

1880–1887 ▶ Attends grammar school in Iglau

1887–1891 ▶ Attends the construction department of the industrial school in Brünn

1887–1892 ▶ Practical training in the planning department of the armed forces in Würzburg

1892–1895 ▶ Hoffmann studies architecture at the Academy of Fine Arts in Vienna under Carl von Hasenauer and Otto Wagner.

1895 ▶ Co-founds the avant-garde "Sevener's Club" (with Joseph Maria Olbrich and Koloman Moser and others)

1895–1896 ▶ Study trip to Italy

1897 ▶ Begins working at Otto Wagner's studio in Vienna. Hoffmann co-founds the Vienna Secession.

1898 ▶ Marries Anna Hladik
Two apartment houses in Vienna I
Installation design for the Vienna Secession I exhibition
"Viribus unitis" room of the "Education" pavilion at the 1898 Vienna Anniversary exhibition
Installation design for the Vienna Secession II exhibition

1899 ▶ Both Hoffmann and Koloman Moser receive professorships at the School of Applied Arts (today the University of Applied Arts) in Vienna. Hoffmann teaches in the architecture, metalworking, enameling, and arts and crafts departments.

Installation design for the Vienna Secession III exhibition
Anteroom and secretary's office of the Secession Building, Vienna I
Installation design for the Vienna Secession IV exhibition
Installation design for the Vienna Secession V exhibition (including the "Ver sacrum" hall)
Furnishings for the Vienna branch of the firm Apollo, Vienna I
Remodeling of Paul Wittgenstein's country house, Bergerhöhe near Hohenberg, Lower Austria
Exhibition design for the firm Popischil at the World's Fair in Paris, 1900

1900 ▶ Birth of son Wolfgang
Exhibition of the School of Applied Arts and Secession at the World's Fair in Paris, 1900
Forestry office with residence for the Wittgenstein forestry commission, Hohenberg, Lower Austria
Installation design for the Vienna Secession VIII exhibition (Applied Arts)
Moser-Moll double house, Hohe Warte, Vienna XIX
Henneberg residence, Hohe Warte, Vienna XIX

1901
Installation design for the Vienna Secession XII exhibition
Friedrich Victor Spitzer residence, Hohe Warte, Vienna XIX

1902
Installation design for the Vienna Secession XIV exhibition
Installation design for the Vienna Secession Art exhibition in Düsseldorf
Remodeling of Max Biach's house, Vienna IV
Protestant church and vicarage, St. Aegyd am Neuwald, Lower Austria

1903
Founding of the Wiener Werkstätte (Vienna Workshops)
Installation design for the Vienna Secession XVII exhibition
Installation design for the Vienna Secession XVIII exhibition (Gustav Klimt)
Labor union hotel of the Poldi Ironworks (Poldihütte), Kladno, Bohemia

Country house for Anton Knips, Seeboden, Carinthia

1904
Purkersdorf Sanatorium, Lower Austria
Exhibition spaces at the St. Louis World's Fair (USA), 1904
Furnishings for the Flöge fashion salon, Vienna VI
Hunting lodge for Alexander Pazzani, Gröbming, Styria
Remodeling of Wilhelm Figdor's country house, Baden near Vienna, Lower Austria

1905 ▶ Hoffmann leaves the Vienna Secession together with the 'Klimt Group'.
Furnishings for the studio of Gustav Klimt, Vienna
Alexander Brauner residence, Hohe Warte, Vienna XIX
Richard Beer-Hofmann residence, Vienna XVIII
Margarethe Legler residence, Vienna XIX
Palais Stoclet, Brussels

1906
Remodeling of Karl Wittgenstein's hunting lodge, Hochreith near Hohenberg, Lower Austria
Studio addition for Magda Mautner von Markhof, Vienna III
Furnishings for the Berlin branch of the firm Kohn
Hochstetter House, Hohe Warte, Vienna XIX
Carl Moll residence, Hohe Warte, Vienna XIX

1907
Exhibition spaces for Gustav Klimt and the Wiener Werkstätte, International Art Exhibition, Mannheim
Interior design cabaret Fledermaus, Vienna I
Furnishings for the branch office of the publishers K. K. Hof- und Staatsdruckerei, Vienna I

1908
Installation design for International Baukunst exhibition, Vienna (with Josef Hackhofer)
Overall planning and design for the reception hall, the Wiener Werkstätte room, and a small country house for the beechwood firm Kohn at the Kunstschau exhibition in Vienna
Furnishings for Carl Otto Czeschka, Hamburg

1908–1910 ▶ Austrian member of the German Werkbund

1909

Installation design for the Austrian Room at the 10th International Art Exhibition, Munich
Street façade of Café Kremser, Vienna I
Remodeling and furnishings of the Pickler residence (with Karl Bräuner), Budapest
"Portable Hunting Lodge" for Alexander Pazzani, Klosterneuburg-Weidling, Lower Austria
Eduard Ast residence, Hohe Warte, Vienna XIX

1910

Remodeling of Heinrich Böhler's country house, Baden near Vienna, Lower Austria
Halls of the 'Klimt Group' in the art pavilion at Vienna's 1st International Hunting Exhibition
Austrian Pavilion at the International Art Exhibition in Rome
Otto Böhler residence, Karpfenberg, Styria

1911

Reception hall at the Austrian Arts and Crafts exhibition, Vienna 1911/1912
Gravestone for Gustav Mahler, Grinzing cemetery, Vienna XIX

1912

Austrian Department of Monumental Art, Dresden Art Exhibition
Dining room, Austrian Arts and Crafts spring exhibition, Vienna
Furnishings of the Graben Café, Vienna I
Furnishings of the "Volkskeller" tavern in Hotel Pitter, Salzburg
Villa settlement Kaasgraben, Vienna XIX
Edmund Bernatzik residence, Vienna XIX
Remodeling of the administrative building of the Poldi Ironworks, Vienna III
Remodeling of Hugo Koller's country house, Oberswaltersdorf, Lower Austria

1913

Infirmary of the Bosnian Electric Company, Jajce, Bosnia
Two spaces at the exhibition of the Austrian Wallpaper, Lincrusta and Linoleum Industry in Vienna
Factory building for the firm Günther Wagner, Vienna X
Country house for Otto Primavesi, Winkelsdorf, Moravia

Apartment furnishings for Ferdinand Hodler, Geneva
Remodeling Primavesi banking house, Olmütz, Moravia
Austrian House and the exhibition space for the beechwood firm Kohn, Deutsche Werkbund exhibition in Cologne
House remodeling for Josefine Skywa, Vienna XIII
Josefine Skywa and Robert Primavesi residence, Vienna XIII

1914

Hall and women's salon at the Austrian Arts and Crafts exhibition, Vienna 1913/1914
Design of the Austrian House, International Booksellers and Graphics exhibition, Leipzig

1915

Apartment remodeling for Anton Knips, Vienna VII

1916

Industrial buildings for the Wacker Works, Burghausen am Inn, Germany
Furnishings for Heinrich Böhler's studio, Vienna I
Furnishings for Paul Wittgenstein, Vienna VIII
Furnishings for the office of Rudolf Weinberger, Vienna IV

1917

Austrian Art exhibition in Copenhagen and Stockholm

1919

Alterations on the Pichlmayrgut estate for Alexander Pazzani, Pichl near Schladming, Styria
Remodeling of the Bad Gross Ullersdorf health resort, Czechoslovakia
House of Sigmund Berl, Freudenthal, Czechoslovakia

1920 ▸ Appointed official building commissioner for the City of Vienna
Fritz Grohmann residence, Würbenthal-Pochmühl, Czechoslovakia

1921

Remodeling and furnishings of Kuno Grohmann's house, Würbenthal-Pochmühl, Czechoslovakia

1922 ▸ Divorces his wife Anna
House of Karl Dunckel, Budapest
Furnishings for the art dealership of Gustav Nebehay, Vienna I

1923

"Relaxation Room for a Lady", Austrian Arts and Crafts Exhibition, Vienna
Furnishings for the offices spaces of the firm Grohmann, Würbenthal, Czechoslovakia
Gravestone for Eduard Ast, Heiligenstadt cemetery, Vienna XIX
Country house of Eduard Ast, Aue near Velden, on Lake Wörther, Carinthia
Urban housing estate Klosehof, Vienna XIX

1924

Design of two exhibition spaces, Vienna Arts and Crafts Association's anniversary exhibition, Vienna
Fair stand for the firm Grohmann, Reichenberg Fair
Urban housing estate Winarskyhof, Vienna XX
Sonja Knips residence, Vienna XIX
Austrian pavilion at the International Arts and Crafts Exhibition, Paris 1925

1925 ▸ Second marriage to Karla Schmatz, fashion model for the Wiener Werkstätte
Exhibition spaces for the Austrian publishing and reproduction institutions and the Austrian furniture section, International Arts and Crafts Exhibition, Paris 1925

1927

Design of the Austrian section, European Arts and Crafts Exhibition, Leipzig 1927
Sample room for apartment housing in the Viennese community, "Vienna and the Viennese" exhibition
Design of the fair stand for the Italian chamber of commerce, Vienna's Autumn Fair
Design of two exhibition spaces for the "Kunstschau" exhibition, Vienna
Interior design for passenger coaches of the Austrian Federal Railway (with Oswald Haerdtl)

1928

"Tearoom" at "The Modern Apartment" exhibition, Vienna

"Austrian Arts and Crafts, Yesterday and Today" section of the PRESSA international press exhibition, Cologne
Design of two exhibition spaces at the "Art in Industry" exhibition, New York
Furnishings for business space of the confectionery shop Altmann & Kühne on Kärntnerstrasse, Vienna I
Prefabricated house type made of steel for the firm Vogel & Noot, Wartberg, Styria, and Vienna (with Oswald Haerdtl)
Remodeling of Dr. Döll residence
Remodeling of Café Graben, Vienna I
Office spaces for Industria Sarmej S.A., Klausenburg (Cluj-Nápoca), Romania (with Oswald Haerdtl)
Isidor Diamant residence, Klausenburg (Cluj-Nápoca), Romania
Furnishings for the milliner's boutique Tosca, Vienna IV (with Oswald Haerdtl)
Urban housing estate on Laxenburgerstrasse, Vienna X

1929
Remodeling and partial redecorating of the former Skywa-Primavesi residence for Bernhard Panzer, Vienna XIII
Furnishings for the offices spaces of the phonograph company Doblinger (Herzmansky), Vienna I (with Oswald Haerdtl)
"Music Room" exhibition of Viennese installation artists, Vienna
Wiener Werkstätte exhibition space, Austrian Arts and Crafts exhibition, Stockholm
Memorial for Otto Wagner, Vienna I
Overall planning and design of the Austrian Werkbund Exhibition, Vienna 1930

1930 ▶ Appointed honorary citizen of the City of Vienna
Design of the Austrian Werkbund exhibition, Chicago (with Oswald Haerdtl)
Four row houses for the Vienna Werkbund settlement, Vienna XIII

1932 ▶ Bankruptcy of the Wiener Werkstätte. Hoffmann resigns from the Austrian Werkbund
Exhibition design for "The Growing House," Vienna's Spring Fair (with Oswald Haerdtl)
Furnishings for the business space of a branch of

the confectionery shop Altmann & Kühne on Am Graben, Vienna I (with Oswald Haerdtl)
Remodeling and furnishings of Restaurant Hartmann, Vienna I (with Oswald Haerdtl)
Portal and furnishings of the business space for the Ritz perfume shop, Vienna I (with Oswald Haerdtl)
Corner of a living room with a fireplace, Space and Fashion exhibition, Vienna
Furnishings for the commercial space of Adolf Huppert's tailor shop, Vienna I (with Oswald Haerdtl)

1934
Design of the arts and crafts hall at the "Austria in London" exhibition, London
Exhibition design for "50 Years of the Vienna Arts and Crafts Association," Vienna
Portal of the business space of the firm Viktorin, Vienna I (with Oswald Haerdtl)
Furnishings of a wine tavern for Hans Böhler, Baden near Vienna, Lower Austria
"Liberated Craftsmanship" exhibition, Vienna
Austrian exhibition pavilion at the Venice Biennial (with Robert Kramreiter)
Furnishings for the commercial space of the Vadasz Opera perfume shop, Vienna I (with Oswald Haerdtl)

1936 ▶ Emeritus status conferred upon Hoffmann by the School of Applied Arts, Vienna
Integration of a bar at Restaurant Hartmann, Vienna (with Oswald Haerdtl)

1937
"Boudoir d'une grande vedette" for the World's Fair in Paris
Furnishings for the cercle privé of the casino in Baden near Vienna, Lower Austria (with Oswald Haerdtl)
Room furnishings in the Hotel Imperial, Vienna I (with Oswald Haerdtl)

1938
Furnishings for the fashion publications and sewing patterns department of the publishers Otto Beyer, Vienna I (with Oswald Haerdtl)
Remodeling and furnishings of the "House of Fashion" in the Palais Lobkowitz (with Josef Kalbac), Vienna I

1940
Commercial branch of the porcelain manufacturer Meissen, Vienna I (with Josef Kalbac)
Remodeling of the German embassy building to the "Haus der Wehrmacht" (Armed Forces Building), Vienna III (with Josef Kalbac)
Sample apartment for the United Handicraft Workshops of Munich, Munich

1941–1955
During this period, Hoffmann sketches out around 80 never to be built projects, for the most part single-family homes, apartment and country houses, and various exhibition pavilions and gravestone designs.

1945–1956 ▶ Hoffmann renews his Secession membership

1948–1950 ▶ President of the Secession

1949
Urban housing estate on Blechturmgasse, Vienna V

1951
Urban housing estate on Silbergasse, Vienna XIX
Elementary school for girls, Stockerau, Lower Austria

1953
Urban housing estate on Heiligenstädter Strasse, Vienna XIX (with Josef Kalbac)

1956 ▶ Hoffmann dies May 7 in his apartment on Salesianergasse 33, Vienna III.

Map of Vienna

Vienna

1   Spitzer Residence, Steinfeldgasse 4, Vienna XIX
2   Double House for Moser and Moll, Steinfeldgasse 6–8, Vienna XIX
3   Hochstetter House, Steinfeldgasse 7, Vienna XIX
4   Beer-Hofmann Residence, Hasenauerstrasse 59, Vienna XVIII
5   Ast Residence, Steinfeldgasse 2/Wollergasse 12, Vienna XIX
6   Henneberg Residence, Wollergasse 8, Vienna XIX
7   Skywa-Primavesi Residence, Gloriettegasse 18, Vienna XIII
8   Housing Complex Klosehof, Philippovichgasse 1, Vienna XIX
9   Sonja Knips Residence, Nusswaldgasse 22, Vienna XIX
10 Housing Complex Laxenburgerstrasse, Laxenburgerstrasse 94, Vienna X
11 Row Houses at Werkbund Exhibition, Veitingergasse 79–85, Vienna XIII

Purkersdorf

12 Purkersdorf Sanatorium

Bibliography

▸ Josef Hoffmann, Variationen (exhibition catalogue). Mit Beiträgen von Dieter Ronte, Eduard F. Sekler und Hildegund Amanshauser. Vienna: Museum moderner Kunst/Museum des 20. Jahrhunderts, 1987

▸ Vienna 1900: Vienna, Scotland and the European avant-garde. National Museum of Antiquities of Scotland (exhibition catalogue). Edinburgh: Her Majesty's Stationery Office, 1983

▸ Barten, Sigrid: Josef Hoffmann, Wien. Jugendstil und Zwanziger Jahre (exhibition catalogue). Zurich: Museum Bellevue, 1983

▸ Bisanz-Prakken, Marian: Gustav Klimt. Der Beethovenfries; Geschichte, Funktion und Bedeutung. Salzburg: Residenz, 1977

▸ Clair, Jean (ed.): Vienne 1880-1938. L'apocalypse joyeuse (exhibition catalogue). Paris: Centre Georges Pompidou, 1986

▸ Fahr-Becker, Gabriele: Wiener Werkstaette, 1903-1932. Cologne: Taschen, 1995

▸ Gresleri, Giuliano: Josef Hoffmann. New York: Rizzoli 1985

▸ Gorsen, Peter: Josef Hoffmann. Zur Modernität eines konservativen Baumeisters, in: Ornament und Askese, Alfred Pfabigan (ed.). Vienna: C. Brandstätter, 1985, S. 69-92

▸ Hilmes, Oliver: Witwe im Wahn. Das Leben der Alma Mahler-Werfel. Munich: Siedler, 2004

▸ Hoffmann, Josef: Selbstbiographie, in: Ver Sacrum, Neue Hefte für Kunst und Literatur. Vienna/Munich (after 1970)

▸ Kristan, Markus: Josef Hoffmann, Villenkolonie Hohe Warte. Vienna: Album, 2004

▸ Neiß, Herta: 100 Jahre Wiener Werkstätte: Zwischen Mythos und ökonomischer Realität. Vienna: Böhlau 2004

▸ Noever, Peter und Oberhuber, Oswald (ed.): Josef Hoffmann. Ornament zwischen Hoffnung und Verbrechen (exhibition catalogue). Vienna: Österreichisches Museum für Angewandte Kunst/Hochschule für Angewandte Kunst, 1987

▸ Österreichischer Werkbund (ed.): Josef Hoffmann zum 60. Geburtstag. Eine Auswahl seiner Arbeiten anläßlich der Ausstellung im Österreichischen Museum (exhibition catalogue). Vienna: Almanach der Dame, 1930/31

▸ Roth, Alfred: Begegnung mit Pionieren. Le Corbusier. Piet Mondrian. Adolf Loos. Josef Hoffmann. Auguste Perret. Henry van de Velde, Basel/Stuttgart: Birkhäuser, 1973

▸ Sekler, Eduard: Josef Hoffmann: The Architectural Work: Monograph and catalogue of works. Princeton: Princeton University Press, 1985

▸ Toman, Rolf (ed.): Vienna. Art and Architecture, Cologne: Könemann, 1999

▸ Varnedoe, Kirk: Vienna 1900. Art, architecture and design (exhibition catalogue). New York 1986

▸ Witt-Dörring, Christian (ed.): Josef Hoffmann: Interiors, 1902–1913; Munich: Prestel 2006

Credits

▸ Akademie der bildenden Künste, Vienna: 20 above, 25

▸ ©Mark Fiennes/arcaid.co.uk: 12 above

▸ Archiv der Secession, Vienna: 33 both

▸ ©bel etage Kunsthandel GmbH, Wolfgang Bauer: 15 above, 18 below, 20 below, 36 above right, 37 above left, 37 below left, 38 middle left, 38 below, 45 above left

▸ Bildarchiv Foto Marburg: 13 above, 15 below, 52 below, 54, 55, 56 above, 58 all, 59 all, 60, 68, 69

▸ bpk/Staatsbibliothek zu Berlin: 17

▸ ©CORBIS: 7

▸ Das moderne Landhaus und seine innere Ausstattung, Munich 1904: 9 above, 28 both, 29 below, 30, 31 both

▸ Johanna Fiegl: 22, 62

▸ Fondazione La Biennale di Venezia – ASAC: 91 above

▸ gettyimages/Imagno: 70 above

▸ Gössel und Partner, Bremen: 95

▸ Archiv Peter Gössel: 56 below, 79 above

▸ ©Angelo Hornak, London: 57

▸ Photo Franz Hubmann: 61

▸ Innendekoration XIII, 1902: 27 above

▸ Innendekoration XLV, 1934: 90

▸ Das Interieur XIII, 1912: 71

▸ ©János Kalmár, Vienna: 73 below, 82 above

▸ Galerie Yves Macaux: 44 above

▸ Galerie Yves Macaux/Philippe de Formanoir: 40 above right, 40 below, 45 below, 49 below, 70 below

▸ Galerie Yves Macaux/Jacques Vekemans: 44 below

▸ MAK – Österreichisches Museum für angewandte Kunst/Gegenwartskunst, Vienna: 4, 8, 9 below, 10 above, 12 below, 13 below, 14, 16 above, 18 above, 21, 24, 29 above, 34, 35 above, 36 above left, 39, 40 above left, 40 above middle, 42 all, 43 right, 48 above, 49 above, 50, 51, 52 above, 53, 63 both, 64, 65 both, 66 above, 67 above, 73 above, 77 above, 83, 84, 85

▸ ©Georg Mayer/MAK: 36 below both, 37 above right, 37 below right, 38 above, 38 middle row center, 41 all, 43 left, 45 above right, 66 below, 76, 77 below, 82 below, 89 both

▸ ©Fritz Simak/MAK: 67 below

▸ ©Gerald Zugmann/MAK: 16 below

▸ Österreichische Galerie Belvedere, Vienna: 32

▸ Bildarchiv Österreichische Nationalbibliothek, Vienna: 2, 10 below, 11, 19, 72, 74, 87, 88 both

▸ Profil II, 1934: 91 below

▸ ©Margherita Spiluttini, Vienna: 46, 47, 75 both, 86

▸ ©Rupert Steiner, Vienna: 26, 27 below, 78, 79 below, 80 both, 81

▸ Collection of the Toyota Municipal Museum of Art, Tokyo: 38 middle right, 48 below

▸ V & A Images/Victoria and Albert Museum, London: 6, 35 below

The Author

Born in 1956, August Sarnitz is an architect and professor of architectural history and theory at the Vienna Academy of Fine Arts. Studies at the Technical University in Vienna and the Vienna Academy of Fine Arts. Post-graduate studies at the Massachusetts Institute of Technology (M.I.T.). Mr. Sarnitz taught as a guest professor at numerous universities, among them the University of California, Los Angeles, Rhode Island School of Design, Providence, Massachusetts Institute of Technology, and the Royal Academy, School of Architecture, Copenhagen.

The author has published on twentieth-century architecture and exile-architecture in the United States and New Zealand. He has written a number of books including publications on Rudolf M. Schindler (1986), Lois Welzenbacher (1988), Ernst Lichtblau (1994), Ernst Plischke (2003), Adolf Loos (2003), and Otto Wagner (2005).

The author conveys his thanks to all those who assisted in the preparation of the publication. Particular thanks is owed to Dr. Markus Kristan and Eva Santo.